Saying Goodbye to a Baby

Volume I: The Birthparent's Guide to Loss and Grief in Adoption

Patricia Roles

Child Welfare League of America
Washington, DC

CHILD WELFARE LEAGUE OF AMERICA, INC.
440 First Street, NW, Suite 310, Washington, DC 20001-2085

CURRENT PRINTING (last digit)
10 9 8 7 6 5

Cover design by Anita Crouch
Text design by Eve Malakoff-Klein

Printed in the United States of America

ISBN # 0-87868-387-9

Dedicated to All Birthmothers

"A Mother's Love"

She carried a child beneath her heart
How she must have loved her so
She knew that they must be apart
Even as she watched her baby grow
    The swelling of her belly
    The movement felt within
    The time would soon be coming
    When she must give up this, her kin
She struggled with the thoughts inside
The decision she must make
To give this child a chance in life
One she must not take
    The day arrived, a winter day
    The blizzard running wild
    The birthing of her little girl
    Her precious little child
It must have been so very hard
To bear this one and then
Whisper as she's whisked away
"Perhaps we'll meet again"
    The world so cold and lonely
    Arms empty as she leaves
    None can know the special hurt
    And times that she so grieves
To hold the one she gave away
But it had to be for good
She could not care as she would want
Perhaps another would
    Dear mother wherever she may be
    It must have been so hard
    To give her for another to raise
    Her life it will have scarred
As the years go by, she must think
At each and ever year
That special day that she gave birth
And prayed for her daughter so dear
    That day would be etched in her memory forever
    To forget that time and her child? NEVER!
    Is she all right wherever she'll be?
    Perhaps to give anything once just to see
Somewhere in this world a little girl would live
Unaware of what her mother had given
And though it hurt her to the core
She gave her a new life—an open door.
            —Adoptee Jennifer Bige (May 11, 1984)

Contents

viii

Preface

This book is written for all the birthparents with whom I share a common bond of unspoken loss and grief. It was my experience 18 years ago of having placed my baby daughter for adoption that made me aware of the need for such a book. My subsequent training as a social worker enlarged my understanding of birthparents' needs. After writing my first book, *Facing Teenage Pregnancy, A Handbook for the Pregnant Teen,* and giving workshops to groups of professionals on counseling pregnant teenagers, I found each time that someone in the audience would speak up about her own experience with teenage pregnancy and adoption. I also began to receive phone calls and letters from distressed birthparents and had nowhere to refer them for help. Eventually, I began leading counseling groups for birthparents through a local family service agency and began to see how vast were the unaddressed needs and pain of birthparents.

The personal excerpts throughout the book were given to me by three birthparents—Donna, Sue, and Pauline—who attended my counseling groups. Their expression of their feelings and the reality of their experiences greatly enrich this book, and I am very appreciative.

This book grew out of my identification of birthparents' needs. There is an ample supply of books on loss and grief in death, divorce, and separation, but only a chapter or article here and there about birthparents' grief. Grief following death is like that experienced in relinquishment, but there are significant differences. The discussion about grief in this book pertains specifically to relinquishment for adoption and takes these differences into account.

Society does not recognize the right of birthparents to grieve. It is only recently that professionals in the field of adoption have begun to realize and acknowledge that a grief process occurs following relinquishment of an infant. However, I still come across professionals who work in the field of death and dying who look at me with puzzled expressions when I refer to loss in adoption. They do not think of the birthparents' loss when thinking of adoption; they view adoption as the adoptive parents and the adopted child "coming together," without seeing the separation that precedes it.

In reality, all three parties in the adoption triangle experience some kind of loss. The adoptive parents have to deal with their infertility, and mourn their inability to have their own biological child. Adopted children go through the separation from their birthparents early in life. As they become adolescents and adults, they have to deal with the gaps in their knowledge of their own roots, and may interpret their relinquishment as rejection. Loss is only one of the shared themes in adoption.

There are two major reasons that loss through adoption has not been acknowledged or sanctioned by society: (1) the social stigma attached to out-of-wedlock births and teenage pregnancy; and (2) the traditional view that adoption simultaneously meets the needs of all three parties. An irrevocable decision on the part of the birthmother is necessary, and this leaves little incentive to acknowledge her painful feelings. Until recently, birthparents were told that they would forget, would just get on with their lives, and could have other children later on. To acknowledge and encourage the grief reaction might jeopardize the signing of the adoption papers, and might risk disproving the assumption that adoption was the "best" alternative for everyone.

A major shift, however, has taken place in the adoption picture over the last 20 years, influenced by: (1) decreased stigma on single parenting as divorce rates increased; (2) decreased stigma on out-of-wedlock births; (3) the civil rights movement; (4) the women's rights movement; and (5) legalized abortion. In the past, adoption was viewed as the price to be paid for the shame of having an out-of-wedlock child, but today the decision making that birthparents must do has also changed. The reality is that no birthparent ever forgets, nor does he or she desire to forget, the child placed for adoption.

As birthmothers emerge, birthfathers are gradually coming forth. They have begun to demand their rights in the adoption process. Until recently they have largely been left out by birthmothers and adoption agencies. Their emergence has already begun to change the consent process in adoption. This book refers to the experience of both birthmothers and birthfathers through the use of the word birthparents, although the focus will more often be on the birthmothers' situation. The language in adoption can be confusing, because it is difficult to adequately describe its varied relationships, just as in blended families. I chose the term birthparents instead of biological parents because I feel that it most closely defines this particular relationship to the child. The reality is that there are two sets of parents in adoption. Both have valid roles: the ones who nurtured the child during pregnancy, gave birth to the child, and provided the child's genetic and hereditary traits; and the ones who raised the child to adulthood and provided the nurturing environment and relationships. Both are valuable, essential contributions to the child's life. Neither parent is the more real parent. They are just different kinds of parents. Neither set of parents owns the child. The following poem describes the different roles of the birthmother and the adoptive mother in a most beautiful way.

Legacy of an Adopted Child

Once there were two women
Who never knew each other
One you do not remember
The other you call mother
Two different lives shaped to make yours one
One became your guiding star
The other became your sun
The first gave you life
And the second taught you to live in it
The first gave you a need for love
And the second was there to give it
One gave you a nationality
The other gave you a name
One gave you the seed of talent
The other gave you an aim
One gave you emotions
The other calmed your fears
One saw your first sweet smile
The other dried your tears
One gave you up—it was all that she could do
The other prayed for a child
And God led her straight to you
And now you ask me through your tears
The age-old question through the years
Heredity or environment—which are you the product of
Neither my darling—neither
Just two different kinds of love

1
The Adoption Decision

Making a decision about your baby is difficult because this is an emotional decision with lifelong repercussions for you, your unborn child, and others. It helps to discuss your decision with a trained, unbiased counselor who can give you information on *all* the options and help you weigh them. The most important part is that this be your decision without pressure from others, because it is you who will have to live with the decision, not those around you. All too many birthparents have felt that they were deprived of choice because of pressures from family, friends, doctors, social workers, and society. It can still happen.

When unwanted pregnancy occurs, there are stages you will go through.

- *Shock* is the first stage, when you first realize that you are pregnant. You wonder "why me?" Of course, it "couldn't happen to me!" You are flooded with feelings of fear, panic, anger, sadness, guilt, despair, or desperation. Emotions can be overwhelming. You should be aware that depression and thoughts of suicide can arise, so be sure to find someone to support you through this difficult time. If you have no one to turn to, call your local crisis line for help. You will need time to grasp what is happening.

- *Denial*—thinking and acting as if something does not exist—is a common experience and an important defense against emotional pain. You may try to put off the inevitable for as long as possible. Denial is useful only for a short while, however, to give you time to sort out your feelings and thoughts. Denial of the pregnancy prevents you from exploring the alternatives. Prolonged denial can limit the options open to you. For example, abortion can usually be performed only up to around 20 weeks of preg-

1

nancy; and early abortion, during the first 12 weeks, is less traumatic than late abortion. Denial of your pregnancy also interferes with getting adequate prenatal care, which may affect your unborn child, as well as leaving you with guilt feelings later in life.

- *Facing the facts* is inevitable. Before you can accept your pregnancy you may do a great deal of crying. You may fear what is ahead, but once you accept your pregnancy then you can begin to plan for the future. Facing the facts means telling those around you. You can then allow people to reach out to you and help you through this difficult time.

- *Decision making* occurs as you think through the various alternatives open to you. There is no easy answer; all the choices are difficult. You will need to find out as much as possible about all of them and examine both the immediate and long-term consequences of each choice. Reaching a decision helps bring order out of the confusion that you have experienced until this point. When seeking help, be sure that the counseling agency you go to does not have a bias in its mandate. Some agencies are funded to "counsel to" a particular option, and are not free to discuss all the options with you, particularly abortion.

Basically, there are four alternatives to choose from: (1) single parenting; (2) marriage or living in a common-law relationship; (3) abortion; and (4) adoption. Adoption is discussed in this book; the other three are discussed in my first book, *Facing Teenage Pregnancy—A Handbook for the Pregnant Teen.*

Exploring Adoption

Adoption refers to the process by which the legal relationship between the parents and the child is transferred permanently by judicial order from the biological parents to the adoptive parents. Each state and province has its own adoption legislation. They vary in the number of days after birth that adoption consents may be signed. *No adoption consent may be signed before the birth of the child!* Jurisdictions vary in the time periods for withdrawal of the consent to adoption. Be sure to understand the process and each document before you sign any papers. You are entitled to legal counsel if you are unsure of your rights. Be absolutely sure of your decision before signing any adoption papers because you may not have the option of revoking your consent. Even if there is a process in your province or state for withdrawal of consent, the judge looks at the best interests of the child. If the child has been in the adoptive home for a period of time and the adoptive parents' lifestyle is more stable than yours, a judge might not allow your decision to be revoked.

Think everything through carefully. Do not let anyone rush you—you do not have a time limit in which to sign the papers. The time period is there only to ensure that you do not sign the adoption consent too soon after birth, because this is an emotional time and birthparents often change their minds once they experience the actual birth of the child. A preliminary decision for adoption may be made during the pregnancy, but cannot be made definite until after you give birth. If you need time after delivery to think everything through, you can have your baby placed temporarily in a foster home where you can visit your baby and take time to make your decision.

Once the adoption consents are signed, there is a probationary period before the adoption is legalized. This time varies from state to state and province to province but is on average about six months. Usually a social worker visits the adoptive parents during this period before the final adoption order is granted.

The consent of the birthmother must always be obtained for adoption to proceed; no one can sign on your behalf, even if you are a minor. More recently, birthfathers are being asked for their consent where possible. Again this varies from place to place.

Open and Closed Adoption

In agencies where openness exists, the degree of openness varies. Open adoption is a term that refers to the exchange of information (usually identifying) between birthparents and adoptive parents, and to the possible opportunity for face-to-face contact among birthparents, adoptive parents, and child.

The extent of openness may include:

- receiving identifying information
- meeting each other
- having adoptive parents present at the delivery
- actually handing your child into the arms of the adoptive parents
- continuing exchange of information after placement (letters and photos)
- continuing contact with the child

Opposite to openness is traditional closed adoption, which refers to the maintenance of confidentiality of both the birthparents and adoptive parents. No identifying information is exchanged, though both parties are able to obtain nonidentifying information. The birthparents may be given nonidentifying profiles of a number of adoptive families and be offered their preference. There may be the opportunity to exchange letters, pictures, and mementos before the birth of the child; sometimes adoptive parents agree to exchange letters and pictures after the child is placed with them, but there is no guarantee that this will occur. In many states the opportunity now exists to sign a waiver of confidentiality at the time of the adoption. This permits identifying information to be released if the adopted child, upon reaching the age of majority, seeks information about the birthparents.

It is important to ensure that the nonidentifying information about the adoptive family is given to you in writing. You may want to look back at it later on when time clouds memories. You may not think that you will need it in writing, but later in life you may be looking for any available mementos or details. If you have placed a child for adoption in the past and never received a written profile of the adoptive family, you can write to the adoption agency and request the nonidentifying information.

Be sure to check the options open to you in your province or state. If open adoption is a possibility, you will have to think through the degree of openness that you can handle. Openness is not something that every birthparent is comfortable with. Some people are comfortable meeting adoptive parents and even having them present at the delivery. For others, this is too much contact because this is their only chance to be alone with their child, to nurture their child, and to say good-bye. Some mothers may need this time to think through their decision to be sure it is the right path to take. If birthparents agree to meet the adoptive parents too soon, or to have them present at the delivery, they may not feel free to change their mind lest they disappoint the adoptive parents after getting their hopes up. These are all highly personal decisions and each person is different. There is no right or wrong way.

Routes to Adoption

Basically, there are two types of adoption: (1) public agency or voluntary agency adoption; and (2) private or independent adoption.

Agency Adoption

Agency adoption refers to social agencies that are licensed and regulated by the state or province to facilitate the adoption process. The agency will have counselors who meet with prospective adoptive parents and provide an assessment called a home study. The counselors are also available to help you weigh decisions and provide emotional support. Agencies vary in their degree of openness in the adoption process. Agency adoptions may have a religious affiliation. In the United States, you can locate a licensed adoption agency by contacting your state department of social services, the Child Welfare League of America, or the Family Service Association. In Canada, contact your provincial ministry of social services or Children's Aid Society.

Private or Independent Adoption

Private or independent adoption refers to adoptions that take place as the result of collaboration between the birthparents and a private intermediary. Private or independent adoptions are not legal in all states or provinces. The intermediary may be a lawyer, physician, or independent adoption facilitator. They do not necessarily have counseling skills and are not primarily there to assist you in decision making, because they are often working on behalf of prospective adoptive parents. Many adoptive parents are desperate to find a baby through adoption, and there may not be an unbiased home study of the adoptive parents. Be sure to check out the person you are dealing with.

Adoptive parents may be paying a substantial sum of money to the intermediary to facilitate an adoption. It is an offense to give or receive payment either directly or indirectly for the procurement of a child for adoption. Some adoption facilitators advertise attractive packages to locate birthparents, including payment of medical expenses, living expenses and allowances, or flights to another state. Others provide birthparents with flexibility in the degree of openness, which can seem very attractive to birthparents. Many licensed agencies are now also offering a similar degree of openness. Some birthparents like private or independent adoption because they have more control over the process. Birthparents should also seek counsel from their own lawyer to represent their interests in the adoption. It is important that the adoptive parents cover all of your legal costs in connection with the adoption.

Making and owning your decision for adoption is a step that helps you begin and later get through the grief process. This initial grieving, which begins before the birth of your child, is referred to as anticipatory grief. You will begin to think ahead to the loss and will need to plan for this process.

Once A Child

For Monica, from Her Birthmother

We've grown together for two years.
We've shared together your laughter and tears.
Since your first moments in this world
So many, many things have unfurled.
　　　Once a child, you're grown now.
　　　The time has come to pass.
　　　Know I'll always love you.
　　　That's all I'll ever ask.
You've had the time to live and grow.
How was I to ever, ever know
I couldn't give the care that you would need.
Mine wouldn't be the voice that you would heed.

When I had to say good-bye to you
I didn't know how much that I'd go through
Wanting to be with you all the while.
I pray you have someone to care
And friends that always, always will be there
A family to support you all the time
Who give the love I long to give a child of mine.

—Imelda Buckley

2
The Pregnancy and Birth Experience

The Pregnancy

The first important step is to confirm that you are in fact pregnant and not worrying needlessly. Home pregnancy tests can give you a false positive reading so be sure to have another test done by your pharmacy, medical clinic, or family doctor. This involves giving them a urine sample to analyze.

It is often assumed that pregnancy is a happy time. An unwanted pregnancy, however, added to the emotional and physical changes usual during pregnancy, can be an overwhelming experience. This is likely your first pregnancy. First pregnancies are scary to all women.

If you are a teenager, then you are already in the midst of physical and emotional changes. During adolescence your body needs extra nutrients for growth, and pregnancy will add demands on your system. Your hormonal level changes during adolescence and even more so with pregnancy.

Pregnancy can be a time when moods can fluctuate from laughing one moment to crying the next moment. It is normal to feel anxious as well as high during pregnancy. It is also natural to feel curiosity and excitement as a life grows inside. Even if the pregnancy is unwanted, you will find some positive times in the experience, and you will learn a great deal.

It is common to have fears about pregnancy and childbirth. All women experience fears even when the pregnancy is planned and wanted. Most fears are about unknowns such as labor and delivery. You can prepare for stages of pregnancy and childbirth by reading material from the library, from your family doctor, from the public health nurse, from prenatal classes, and from women who have given birth. Remember though, that many women focus on the difficulties. Pregnancy and delivery are different for every individual.

Prenatal classes offer instruction about labor and delivery. Classes are available through your local public health department.

9

If you are a teenager and self-conscious about going to a prenatal class with older, married women, ask your family doctor or teen clinic if there are any classes for pregnant teenagers in your area. If not, or if you feel uncomfortable attending a group, your local public health nurse would be able to provide information about labor and delivery, as would your family doctor. It helps to have a support person with you during the labor and delivery. This person would be called your "labor coach" and could attend the prenatal classes with you. If you do not have a family member, boyfriend, or friend to be with you, a volunteer labor coach may be arranged. Check with the hospital social worker, adoption agency, or public health nurse. It is also advisable that you tour the hospital where you will deliver, to become familiar with the surroundings and procedures ahead of time, so that there are fewer unknowns.

> *Pauline:* I put on little weight so I was able to keep my pregnancy a secret. At seven months, I left town to stay with a girlfriend. My delivery was very painful, long, and lonely. I had no support person during or after the delivery.

During the pregnancy you will have many bodily changes. You will gain around 25 pounds over the nine-month period. A well-balanced diet is important for your health and for your unborn child. You will have to watch that you do not gain too much weight; it can be difficult to take the pounds off after the baby's birth. Stretch marks are left on the skin as it expands with the rapid increase in size. The more weight you gain, the more stretch marks you will be left with. Moisturizing cream and exercise can help your skin retain its elasticity, but you will likely be left with some stretch marks on your breasts, stomach, hips, and thighs. They will gradually fade with time. As your body changes shape, you will no longer be able to fit into your favorite clothes. You will need loose, comfortable clothing.

You will need plenty of rest and will feel quite tired, especially during the first three months and near the end of your pregnancy. However, exercise is important. Carry on your life as normally as possible, but avoid any activity in which there is a risk of falling or injury.

Constipation is common during pregnancy. A diet with fluids, grains, fruits, and vegetables, as well as exercise and relaxation, can help. Your diet is especially important; you have a baby growing inside you who needs adequate nutrition for healthy development. If you are an adolescent, your body already requires additional nutrients for your own growth. You will find books in the library about nutrition and pregnancy. Your family doctor and public health department will also have booklets available.

Your breasts will gradually increase in size and may be tender to the touch. A good support bra can help. Your nipples will become darker, and there may be a discharge. This is in preparation for nursing. Some birthparents choose to breast-feed their babies, and if you plan to do so you should learn more about breast-feeding from your doctor or public health nurse. Your library will have books on the subject.

Nausea and vomiting, referred to as "morning sickness," often occur during the first three months. Small frequent meals, dry crackers and clear tea with lemon juice, and avoidance of fatty foods might help. This is a temporary problem, but if it persists or vomiting becomes severe, see your doctor.

Backache is common later in pregnancy, because the extra weight changes your body posture and puts added strain on your lower back. Your doctor or health nurse can provide you with exercises that can help.

Swelling of the feet and ankles is a common problem. Rest with your feet up, and notify your doctor if it persists or if your hands and face swell up as well.

Take time to understand the process that your body is going through. Ask questions. You have as much right to know what happens during pregnancy as any mother who is keeping her child. It is your body, and your chance to provide the best you can for your child during the months of growth within the womb. Do not underestimate your role in your child's life. You are nurturing your child in his or her earliest months before birth, during delivery, and in the first few days of life. You are providing the child with his or her genetic makeup. Heredity plays an important part in any person's life. You have a legitimate and an important role as the birthmother of your child. Regular medical checkups are important during the pregnancy to monitor your health and your baby's health. Alcohol, smoking, and drugs endanger your baby's life. You must not take any medication—not even aspirin—during pregnancy without the doctor's consent. Birthparents often wish they had appreciated this limited time they had with their babies, and wish they had given their children more during the pregnancy and in the first few days of life.

Begin thinking about giving your child his or her birth name during the pregnancy. There are books in libraries and bookstores that have lists of possible names. Although this name will most likely be changed by the adopting parents, it is still an important step in your child's life. It will be the name placed on your child's original birth certificate. Don't save the name for your next child. It belongs to this child. Your next child will have another name because he or she will be a different child, not a replacement for this baby. Names are also important so that you can connect your memories of the child to a name. You will have a name to use when referring to him or her.

During the pregnancy, begin planning the degree of contact you want to have with your baby after delivery. Remember that until you sign the adoption consent forms, you are the parent and guardian of the child. You are entitled to see your baby, breast-feed or bottle-feed your baby, and care for your baby in any way you wish. Some birthparents buy a special outfit or special toy to go with the baby. The degree of contact is a personal decision, and varies from person to person. Some birthparents cannot handle holding or feeding the baby because they fear they will not be able to separate when it comes time to leave the hospital. If you choose no contact, you should not feel guilty, because it may be the best way for you to cope with the separation and loss. Just remember that you have the choice, and it is for you to decide, not for others to impose their views upon you. You have the same rights that every mother has.

Some birthparents look back with regret at not having seen their baby. It is more difficult to grieve the loss of someone whom you have not seen. Some women regret not having held the baby, and wish they had taken advantage of this short time together to say goodbye. Take the time to think these decisions through so that you will feel more in control of the events ahead.

The Birth

"Labor" is the term given to the process your body goes through before delivery of the baby. About two weeks before the onset of labor the baby's position drops lower in your abdomen. The baby is settling into the birth position. You may need to urinate more often as the baby presses on your bladder.

You will recognize the beginning of labor by the contractions—tightening of the abdominal muscles—that gradually become stronger and stronger. They feel like cramps. When the cramps are regular, and last about 30 seconds each, and are spaced about eight minutes apart, it is time to call your doctor and go to the hospital. You may have a blood-tinged vaginal discharge or a gush of clear fluid from the vagina. Go to the hospital if you have any of these signs because they mean that labor is under way. You should not eat or drink anything from now on, because you may have to have an anesthetic at the hospital.

Babies do not always arrive on time. You should have a bag packed in advance so that you are ready to go to the hospital at any time. Babies might be born a couple of weeks early or late. Once you get to the hospital, you will be brought to a labor room. You can have someone with you in the labor room. You will stay in the labor room until the cervix is dilated, and the baby is ready to be born. You may be given an enema to clean out your bowel. Your genital area will be swabbed with disinfectant. Nurses and doctors will be in and out of the labor room monitoring your condition. Pain medication may be given as needed, but it is necessary that you be alert in order to help in the birth of your baby by pushing and relaxing as instructed during delivery.

You may give birth in the labor room or may be taken to the delivery room where various types of anesthesia are available. You should discuss this with your doctor ahead of time. The doctor may have to do an episiotomy—a small cut requiring a few stiches—to allow the baby's head to come out easily.

If your pelvis is too small to allow a vaginal delivery, or there are other unforeseen complications, a cesarean birth may be necessary. A so-called cesarean section involves surgery to remove your baby through the abdomen. This leaves a small scar on your abdomen.

When your baby is born, you will have the first opportunity to see and hold him or her. You may or may not be very alert at this time; some mothers feel quite alert. You will be taken to a room in the hospital, ordinarily a shared room, possibly with other mothers who are keeping their babies. If you are concerned about sharing a room, you should discuss this with your doctor ahead of time.

You will need to prepare yourself for questions asked by other patients. They will not know that you are planning to place your baby for adoption and may ask about your husband, or ask other uncomfortable questions. You can decide how much or how little information about yourself you wish to disclose.

You might ask your nurse if there are any other mothers on the floor who are placing their children for adoption; there might be someone in the same situation with whom you might talk. I have known of birthmothers who were not told about others on the same floor who were placing their babies for adoption and were denied the opportunity of this special type of support. If you don't ask, you might not find out!

> *Donna*: My son arrived right on schedule. He was big, healthy, and beautiful. It was a wonderful day. All worries, biases, and fears were laid aside by everyone. His birth gave everyone so much happiness. I was very proud of my accomplishment. Bringing a life into the world is truly a blessed event. I took great joy and pride in taking my visitors to the nursery to show them my baby boy. Sometimes I would go to the nursery just to look at him. Sometimes I'd talk to him through the glass just so he'd know how much I loved him. The nurses bent the rules and asked me if I wanted to come into the nursery to hold him. I went in, but I couldn't touch him. I was afraid that if I touched him I would never let go. I wish now that I had held my baby. He should have been allowed the vital experience of having had his mother's arms around him in those first few days after birth. If I could give advice to any birthmother placing her child for adoption, I would recommend that mother and child have that special time together before they are separated.

> Despite all the joy of the arrival of my beautiful baby, there were certain unpleasant events at the hospital that should not go unmentioned. I was placed in a room with three other women who were keeping their babies. They would hold their babies, nurse them, diaper them, and share them with their husbands. I asked my doctor to be moved to another room, but apparently there was no other available space for me. The other mothers who shared my room were not informed of my status. I had to explain why my

"husband" had not been in to see me. I suppose that I could have lied, but that didn't seem to be the right thing for me to do. After my reunion, 16 years later, I became aware that there was another young woman on the same floor at that time who was placing her baby for adoption as well. Amazingly, no one mentioned this. Didn't anyone on the hospital staff understand how much comfort we could have given each other?

In the days following the delivery, you will feel tired. Your abdomen will feel sore for a couple of weeks, and it will be uncomfortable to sit down. A warm bath will feel soothing. You will need to wear a sanitary pad because you will bleed from the vagina for a few weeks. Sanitary pads are recommended rather than tampons, to reduce the risk of infection.

Your breasts will ache. If you are not breast-feeding, you will be given a series of injections to stop the production of milk. You will need a tight support bra during this time to ease discomfort. Limiting fluid intake can also help. There will also be some discharge from your breasts until the milk production ceases. After the delivery, some mothers may continue to feel sensations as if the baby is still kicking in the womb. If this happens, you are not going crazy! Don't be afraid of this. Just remember the good feelings associated with those sensations.

Your emotions will be up and down during your hospital stay. After the delivery is a vital time to reflect and rethink your decision now that your baby is a reality. You must not accept pressure from others to follow the decision you made before the baby's birth. If you are having doubts, take the time you need to confirm your decision. Do not rush to make the decision just because you are being discharged from the hospital. The baby can be placed in a foster home to allow you the time to make up your mind. If you feel depressed (discussed later in "Postpartum Blues and Depression"), you should not sign any legal document.

Your time with your child in the hospital is your own. Use this time to say goodbye to your baby in any way that you wish. Some birthparents have a special ceremony in the hospital chapel. There are chaplains available in all hospitals to talk with you and plan such a service. You might want your child baptized. You might want a special moment alone with your baby.

You are also entitled to mementos from the hospital, such as the baby's medical bracelet. You can take pictures or cut a lock of hair. You can take a set of handprints or footprints in plaster. Jot down some vital details such as time of birth and height and weight, and get copies of the hospital records. Talk with your nurse and take note of any information, because you won't want to forget it later on. All these details are important to remember this special event in your life. You will want any concrete evidence of your child's existence to confirm that he or she was part of your life.

You will need to complete a form to register your child's birth with his or her birth name. You can also photocopy this as a memento.

There may be other people who would like to see your baby and say their goodbyes, such as the birthfather or your parents. This child may be the first grandchild in the family, and may hold a special place in your parents' lives. Think about the significant people whom you want to notify of the birth of your baby. It is a two-way process. If you do not inform them, they will not be able to provide needed support. It is a time when you will need as much support as possible.

Leaving the hospital without your baby will feel as though you are leaving empty-handed. It will feel as if a part of you is being left behind. You carried the baby for nine months and now you are alone once again. You will probably have some feeling of relief that the labor and delivery are all over, but you will not forget, nor will you want to forget, your baby. Life goes on, and so will yours, but something will be different. You have just experienced both a miracle and a loss at the same time. Allow yourself time to heal, not just physically but emotionally as well.

3
Loss and Grief: Aspects of the Normal Grief Reaction

Relinquishing a child for adoption is a major loss. Grief is a normal reaction to that loss. Grief is defined in the dictionary as deep sorrow, suffering, pain, and distress.

The expression of grief is the beginning of a healing process. This process is different for everyone. You will pass through various stages in the grief process. Some stages might not occur for years after the loss through adoption, especially if you have blocked out your feelings, or have not had the opportunity to express your grief. Your grief process may then be triggered by events later in life such as another loss, birth of another child, marriage, a friend's pregnancy, or menopause.

Some birthmothers seem to be coping well for many years, but then find themselves reliving the past experience of the loss, which may have been triggered by another loss or change in their lives. This is a normal experience, but the intensity of the feelings connected with this experience will depend upon whether you have had the opportunity to grieve the loss at the time, or whether you have denied the feelings in order to cope over the years. If you have held in all your feelings for years, the feelings later in life can be overwhelming. In many persons the grief has been masked as depression or other symptoms, and then unresolved grief is discovered as they begin to deal with the depression.

> *Sue*: Some years were easier. Now that I have reached age 40, and my daughter is of legal age, it has come rushing back to me in a different way.

Grief is something that you cannot afford to avoid unless you are willing to pay the price. To numb yourself to life's pain also means that you numb yourself to life's joy and excitement. The price birthparents pay can be high indeed.

Loss and grief in adoption are like other kinds of loss but are also unique, particularly because the element of decision making is an important aspect of this grief process. First, the more clear it is that the decision is your own, the more you can take the responsibility for it and the less you will get caught up in blaming others. Blaming someone else will block or hinder your ability to get through the grief process. Second, the element of choice in the decision seems to be a factor in society's lack of recognition of the grief that relinquishment causes.

Although many birthparents do feel that they do not have the right to grieve the loss because it was their choice, this is not true when one compares loss in adoption to loss in separation and divorce. Whether a person has choice in regard to a loss has no impact on his or her need to grieve the loss. So you must remember that you have the right to grieve the loss of your baby. More importantly, you must grieve if you are to restore balance to your physical and emotional health; grief is part of a natural healing process.

> *Donna*: I did not know that it was okay for me to feel loss and grief until I became involved in a birthparent workshop. There was a part of me that was very sad for 16 years, but I could not admit why. Now that I have learned to face and deal with that grief, it does not hurt so much.

In adoption there are no public sanctions or public rituals to assist and encourage birthparents' mourning. With a loss through death there are funerals, announcements in the paper, letters of sympathy, flowers, memorial services, social gatherings, religious services, and prayers. In adoption the loss is secret, and mourning is usually private and not necessarily shared by others in the family, let alone through public rituals.

Rituals help us say goodbye to loved ones. They can be as simple as singing a song, reading a poem, or saying a prayer for your baby. A simple ceremony held in a person's home or in a hospital chapel may be a helpful way of saying goodbye to your baby. This is a positive step in acknowledging that adoption is an important transition in birthparents' lives. Children can also be christened or baptized during the time before the adoption consent forms are signed. There are usually chaplains available at all hospitals to provide such services, or to say prayers. They could help you plan a ceremony or service to help you say goodbye in your own way to your baby.

There is room to build some social rituals into the adoption process to decrease the secrecy and allow for public acknowledgment of the loss. Until the public acknowledges the loss as legitimate, it will be hard for birthparents to see their loss as legitimate, and recognize their right to grieve.

The birthparents need to feel connected with the baby before they can accept the separation; there must be some connection to let go of. In the past, babies were often whisked away before mothers could see them. Many birthparents were left with no way to say goodbye to the baby, whom they were not even allowed to acknowledge. It was once thought that birthparents would forget. Professionals now recognize, however, that attachment and bonding take place during pregnancy, and they have realized that it is psychologically important for birthparents to see their child and say goodbye.

It is normal for a grieving person to become preoccupied with objects belonging to, given by, or associated with the lost person. These mementos are cherished, and sorting through them promotes crying and expression of grief, and a gradual desensitization to the loss. In adoption there are few mementos, but it can help to gather whatever you can. These reminders may help to validate that the baby did exist, and the loss did occur. Some individuals do find it just too painful to go through the process of collecting reminders of the baby. However, most birthparents who look back regret not having mementos.

Loss in adoption is a private and often secret affair. This means that social support for birthparents is lacking. The need for social support is amply recognized at the time of loss through death or separation. Family and friends often drop by to help with practical tasks, or just to be there for emotional support.

No flowers or letters of condolence arrive for birthparents. Even if family and friends are aware of the adoption, they likely do not realize the impact of the loss because it is only recently that people are beginning to see relinquishment as a loss. But even if they do recognize the impact of the loss, they do not have any rules as to how they should react to the birthparents. Family and friends may keep away because they are uncomfortable and do not know what to do or say. Many birthparents return home and try to act as if nothing has changed, but a lot has changed. It is a time of major adjustment.

Pauline: Because my pregnancy was a secret, there was no possible way for me to work through my grief. I kept my secret for 11 years and never dealt with the pain of the loss.

Adoption lacks the finality of loss through death. This makes it difficult to mourn because the child still exists, though little may be known about the child's new home and life. Fantasy is then used to fill the gap created by the unknown, and in this way you can maintain your image of the child's life in his new family. Hopes for reunion in the future can also block the acknowledgment of the loss and impair the grief process. Although reunion is a possibility later in life, the loss of the present still exists and needs to be mourned.

There are no rules about how a person is supposed to behave after relinquishing a baby for adoption. With loss through death, it is understood that the bereaved person will likely need some time off work and will not be expected to function as usual at home or at work for a period of time. With loss through adoption, the birthparents are expected to carry on as if nothing has happened. They have to return to work or school right away. Family and friends do not acknowledge that the person is going through a grief process.

If the pregnancy occurs during adolescence, the teenager has to grow up overnight into an adult. She then also has to grieve the loss of her youth, and she often feels that she no longer fits in the world of her peers.

If either of the birthparents was an adopted child, a powerful new dimension is added to the impact of the loss. This baby will likely be their first known blood relative. It will likely bring up feelings and unfinished business related to their own adoption, and, possibly, feelings of having been abandoned by their birthparents.

Another vital point to be conscious of is that this baby cannot be replaced by another baby. Some birthmothers get pregnant again after relinquishing a baby for adoption, in an effort to replace the lost child and to fill the gap in their lives. The loss through adoption leaves you with the sense that part of you is missing. A second baby, however, does not take away the loss of the baby placed for adoption, and does not take away the grief that has to be experienced. So in planning future pregnancies, think through the consequences carefully or you might be setting yourself up for a second loss, or a seriously complicated situation where the second baby cannot live up to your expectations because he or she can never be the lost child.

Other simultaneous losses or changes can make you feel more vulnerable and overwhelmed. Try not to make any major changes during the adjustment period. Birthmothers often leave home, moving away from their family, friends, and familiar daily routines to more unknowns and uncertainties. Running away or leaving your family or home town will not enable you to leave pain behind. In fact, you may cut yourself off from potential social and emotional supports at a time when you need all the support that you can find.

Remember that you grieve because you loved. Many people love and try not to grieve. They try to block out mourning because the feelings can be uncomfortable and overwhelming. Many people fear that if they allow their feelings to be expressed, they will have difficulty controlling a sudden burst of pent-up emotions. Experiencing loss is part of life. Feeling pain means that you are alive. If you can allow yourself to feel its full impact, it will gradually decrease. If you do not allow yourself to feel the pain, it will remain deep inside. Time, in and of itself, does not heal. If you cover up or bury feelings, the grief will not go away. It will just go underground and find other indirect means of expression. Grief is not something that you can afford to postpone.

All people grieve in different ways. Birthmothers may be able to talk more and cry more about the loss than birthfathers. Men may find physical outlets to channel their energy into such as sports or outdoor chores. There is no right or wrong way to grieve. The griever can choose his or her own way of working through the loss.

Experience of Loss: A Framework for Grief

The following grief framework deals specifically with relinquishment for adoption. It describes possible phases you may experience following relinquishment. You may not go through every phase, and you might not go through them in the order they are presented. They are a guide to understanding that your reactions are a normal part of the grief process.

There is no time frame for experiencing these phases of grief. Individuals differ. Events in life can trigger or prevent these different phases. You can use this framework to see what might be ahead, or to understand what you have gone through in the past and where you are at now. You may also find yourself going through similar phases during your pregnancy, before relinquishment.

Numbness and Denial

After relinquishment you will at first feel varying degrees of numbness. You are unable to believe what has happened, and may feel dazed or trancelike. You may feel confused and unable to identify any specific emotions. You may feel robotlike as you carry on your daily routines. Numbness is functional; it allows you to carry on your life without having to accept that anything has changed.

Denial is a refusal to accept what has happened, and is a psychological defense against facing the pain of the loss. Unfortunately, the secrecy in adoption promotes the use of denial and the blocking of thoughts and feelings that often delays the grief process. Denial can be useful and necessary for a short period of time. If it persists, however, you might deny yourself access to all your emotions, including positive ones such as joy and love.

It is common for birthmothers to forget significant events about the birth of the baby, such as date or time, because of the period of numbness or denial. You should not feel guilty if you cannot recall details, because it was necessary for your emotional functioning to use defenses such as denial.

Eruption of Feelings

Your body and mind begin to recognize that change has occurred, and yet you may be trying to carry on as if nothing has happened. Eventually it is no longer possible to pretend, and the eruption of feelings begins. You may experience periodic floods of intense feelings that are not necessarily attached to a particular event. The feelings may come out of the blue. You may feel a wide range of overwhelming emotion: sadness, fear, panic, anger, despair, guilt, and shame. Difficulty sleeping, change in appetite, irritability, fatigue, inability to concentrate, or jumpiness are common occurrences.

The longer these feelings remain unexpressed or suppressed, the greater the fear of loss of control becomes. If you never find an outlet for these feelings, you risk developing symptoms such as nightmares, phobias, sleep disturbances, panic attacks, depression, alcoholism, or drug abuse.

Your body might find physiological outlets for the emotional pain, such as headaches, allergies, muscle tension, digestive disturbances, back pain, or abdominal pain. This does not mean that your physical pain is not real, but that it may be interrelated with the emotional stress and strain. Your body and mind are inseparable. Learn to listen to and understand your body's physical pain because it is an indicator that something is wrong. It takes a tremendous amount of physical and mental energy to keep feelings masked.

Emotions can have uses. For example, anger can help to keep you from facing the loss. The stimulation of intense feelings such as anger keeps you connected emotionally to the child. Dwelling on these intense feelings for too long, however, can do more harm than good.

The expression of emotions brings relief and a certain energy. Try to learn ways to mobilize and channel this energy so that it works with you rather than against you.

Accepting and Owning Your Decision

Accepting your decision is not as easy as it may first appear, because the adoption decision has lifelong repercussions for both you and your child. You are legally and permanently relinquishing parental rights. Even if you hope for a reunion when your child reaches adulthood, you still need to be able to accept that this decision is permanent.

Because the decision is serious, it leads to a lot of rethinking, even long after the adoption papers are signed. It is normal to reevaluate your decision later in life. Hindsight is wonderful! It is natural to wish that you could turn back the clock, but it is impossible to do so.

If you are clear in your decision and can defend it to others, it will be easier to own it and take responsibility for it. Intellectually accepting that the decision was the best option for you at the time, and owning that decision fully, are slightly different. Owning the decision means that you take full responsibility for signing the papers, regardless of the influence of others on your decision.

It means no longer blaming others for the circumstances and the loss. Even if you are being influenced and pressured by social workers, doctors, family, boyfriends, friends, and so-called well-meaning individuals, it will be your signature on the adoption papers, not theirs.

It is understandable that a teenager or young adult would feel intimidated and pressured by those in authority, and would give in to the wishes of someone more powerful, but even a passive decision is a decision in itself. Often this leaves you angry with yourself for allowing yourself to be talked or pressured into a decision against your own beliefs. Many birthparents look back upon their decision and feel angry with having felt powerless then, so now is the time to be be clear about your decision so that you are not left feeling anger at and placing blame on others for years to come. Even anger and blame directed at yourself can prevent you from truly accepting and owning your decision, and keep you locked into a cycle of regret and self-blame.

The adoption system often blocks information available to birthparents, which only adds fuel to the anger birthparents feel. The system of secrecy aids in perpetuating the blame cycle, because it readily gives birthparents a source and target for anger. It is unfortunate that our adoption system keeps birthparents' anger and blame alive by not being sensitive and responding to birthparents' needs.

Searching activity is also a natural part of any grief process, and has been described as occurring during the anger stage. In adoption, however, there are many different types of searching behavior. One kind yields information that will enable you to form a mental picture of your child in order to help you with your feelings. This searching behavior is typical in loss through adoption.

Another type of searching behavior involves scanning faces in a crowd, hoping that you might recognize your child. This is common in adoption, and can be expected because you know that the child is out there somewhere. All these unknowns may make you feel like a detective gathering clues or guessing about circumstances. You will find yourself checking birthdates of children near in age to yours, just in case by chance you might find your offspring. This normal behavior continues throughout life as the child grows.

The most complicated kind of searching is trying to locate the child. Searching for your offspring can be a lengthy, emotional process that involves a great deal of time and energy. Be prepared for varying degrees of success and no guarantee of finding your child. There are organizations to assist people who search for others in the adoption triangle.

Think carefully about the underlying motive behind your need to search. It can stem from unresolved feelings of anger or pain. Some people go into a search with all their energy, leaving grief work on hold. Some bury themselves deeply in the search activity in an effort to fill the gap of the loss in place of feeling the pain.

Following loss through death, some people refuse to believe it and continue to search irrationally for the deceased. In adoption, however, the child is usually still alive and the behavior is not irrational. Some degree of searching activity, even if it remains in your mind rather than an actual activity, is normal for birthparents.

Accommodation and Living with Uncertainty

Once you recognize the loss as real, and you find ways to gradually release your intense emotions, you will not feel as if you have to keep the flood gates up to hold in your feelings. Your thoughts and feelings will be under reasonable control. Accommodating is therefore an indicator that you are learning to live with your decision.

You will continue to experience a range of feelings, but they will surface at appropriate times. For instance, it is normal to expect that you will have an emotional reaction or thoughts about your child on the child's birthday, at Christmas time, or on special occasions. Other events that might stimulate your emotions can include other losses, future pregnancies, pregnancies of family members or friends, or even programs on television or radio that have adoption themes.

It is normal to think about your child, to dream about your child, to dream about reunion, and to develop a fantasy about the child. You will create an image of what you think the child looks like, where he or she is, and what you imagine he or she might be doing. You may know children around the same age and may follow their development with special interest as a guide to understanding what your child might be like.

The nonidentifying information that you can receive from the adoption agency, either at the time of the adoption or later on, can help you build a picture about the child. But whatever your mind creates is only a fantasy, unless you have had the opportunity for firsthand information through open adoption.

Fantasies are normal and decrease the anxiety associated with the unknowns. Excessive fantasies of reunion, however, can lead to false hope, because reunion can be viewed as a means of replacing the loss, and can block the grief process. So the construction of fantasy does not in itself indicate that you have reached the phase of accommodation. Accommodation includes being able to live with the uncertainty ahead.

Living with the unknown has been identified by birthparents as the most difficult part to cope with throughout life. It leaves you in a state of limbo, caught between the hope for reunion and the fear of disappointment and unfulfilled fantasies. You can gather as much information and as many mementos as you can to fill the gaps, but there will still be vast unknown areas, even in open adoption, because you are not the parent in the home with your child. You have chosen not to parent your child for various legitimate reasons, and have to accept that this means living with unknowns and uncertainty. It would be unusual to find a birthmother who would not want to be a fly on the wall in the house of her birthchild.

There are no guarantees that a reunion will take place, and even if it does, it may not take away the unknowns and uncertainty of the intervening years. Reunion may be a possibility, but it is not a certainty that can be planned for. And if reunion does occur, it may happen when you least expect it.

Adopted adults do not necessarily sign up with an adoption registry (described later) as soon as they reach the age of majority. They may never have the desire to meet their birthparents. They may want only information but no contact, or they may not look for birthparents until an event in their own lives precipitates a search (i.e., the birth of their own children or death of their adoptive parents). So, even though legislation is changing to allow reunions to take place, it does not change the uncertainty and unknowns that birthparents must face when a decision for adoption is made. Yearning to be reconnected with the child can be used to deny the reality of the present loss.

Reevaluating and Rebuilding

Reevaluating your feelings about yourself goes on continually. It involves looking at your view of yourself and recognizing that you are a worthwhile, valuable, and caring person. Many birthparents feel so much shame and guilt that they begin to undervalue themselves as individuals.

Birthparents often feel blame for making what they see as a selfish decision. However, all decisions must be made with self in mind. If the decision is made to satisfy someone else, it would not be sound. To place a child for adoption does not mean that you are an unmotherly or uncaring person. In fact, it means that you made a decision based upon your intellect rather than purely on emotion. You tried to make the best decision under the circumstances for both yourself and your baby.

The experience of loss leaves you feeling vulnerable, and self-depreciating thoughts are common. So you have to rebuild your self-confidence. This is the time to put the adoption decision and the loss into perspective and place them appropriately into your life. They represent only one component of your life, not your total life. The past has not changed, but your perception of the past changes over time. It becomes less intense to think about, and your emotions become less intense. It is a time to reach out and rebuild your relationships with others. It is a time to build on your strengths in all parts of your life and to build your supports around you. You will not forget, but memories will gradually become less painful over time. You must move forward with your life.

Because the decision to place a child for adoption has lifelong repercussions, it often leaves birthparents with uncomfortableness and even fear about making other decisions in their lives. It can leave you feeling fearful of other major decisions and commitments, so it is important to rebuild confidence in your own decision-making ability in your adult life. This is something to be aware of and pay attention to because reluctance to make decisions involving commitments could leave you lonely and could block you from experiencing the joys life has to offer.

It is important during the rebuilding to find the circumstances when you experienced personal growth and change on which you can build. You have grown so much from this pain, and it will make you a more sensitive person if you are able to recognize your own strength that helped you cope. It is this same strength that will help you cope with life's other problems.

Positive feelings about yourself do not just happen on their own. You have to be active in building them and in caring for yourself. This means beginning by being nice to yourself and allowing yourself to experience the joys in life. You must believe that you deserve happiness from life and not just sorrow and punishment. The importance of rebuilding your regard for yourself cannot be overemphasized. It is vital to your survival.

Factors That Can Block, Delay, or Prolong Mourning

- Lack of acknowledgment of the loss by society, family, friends, and professionals
- Lack of expression of intense feelings

- Not having a mental image of the baby as a result of lack of information or not having seen the baby

- Preoccupation with the fantasy of reunion in such a way as to avoid dealing with the loss

- Preoccupation with searching for something to fill the gap, to avoid facing painful feelings

- Belief that having a choice takes away the right to grieve

- Self-depreciation and self-blame

- Pressure from others to decide on adoption, which makes it difficult to take responsibility for making a decision

- Lack of support

- Numbing through abuse of alcohol or drugs

- Maintaining secrecy and not acknowledging the loss to yourself or others

In the End

I didn't have the chance to say "Goodbye"
Upon the day
You went away.
> *I didn't want to get into my grief*
> *It came upon me like a thief*
> *Depression and anger had set me aside*
> *Denial had caused me to hide*
I passed that way for many a year
I've loved you through many a tear
I tried so hard to let go of the pain
I tried, but it was in vain
> *And now someone's brought his love to my heart*
> *I'm grieving that we are apart*
> *The pain has been much less since I feel*
> *His love which is helping me to heal*

I want the chance to let you feel my love
Share my peace from God above
I live in hope now that someday you'll see
And in the end you will be free

—Imelda Buckley

Anticipatory Grief

If the decision to place a child for adoption is thought through before the birth, there is time to begin the grief process before the loss actually takes place. "Anticipatory" means to foresee and deal with something in advance. This process is similar to that in loss through death from illness, or in divorce. When a person realizes that the loss is going to happen, there is time to think ahead, prepare, and plan for the loss. You are expecting a loss in the future. As you think through your reaction to the loss, you begin to feel more in control. You may also begin to rehearse and prepare your mind for the events following the birth. As you think ahead, you will begin to experience the feelings associated with loss and grief. You begin working on your grief before the loss actually occurs.

It would be similar to closing your eyes right now and imagining the death of someone you love. It would not take long to evoke intense feelings, even though your loved one has not died. The gradual surfacing of feelings during the time before the loss takes place is the beginning of the grieving process. By accepting your decision and allowing the feelings to surface, you may be reducing the intensity of the flood of feelings later on. You cannot do all your grieving beforehand, but you can certainly go a long way toward taking control of your grief reaction.

If you remain in a state of denial until or after the baby's birth, you will not allow yourself the opportunity of entering the grieving process gradually through anticipatory grief. You will deny yourself the chance to plan your goodbyes to the baby. Your emotions may be more intense if you have not thought about what you can expect to feel.

Even if you are unsure about your decision for adoption, it is still wise to anticipate your reaction and plan for all the possibilities. If you change your mind at the last minute, nothing is lost. In fact, thinking carefully about the loss might help you clarify your decision one way or the other. But you must remember that until the baby is actually born, it is difficult to predict exactly how you will feel.

Understanding Your Grief Reaction

Grieving is a process that you must go through, and feelings are behind your grief. You will experience both physical and emotional responses to your distress, but remember that you are not going out of your mind. It is all a normal healing.

Because the baby is an extension of yourself, you may feel as if you have lost part of yourself. Others may think that you have not developed any strong feelings because you did not parent your child, but this is a false assumption. A powerful sense of union with your child develops during pregnancy and delivery. You have a legitimate relationship with your child. Both you and the baby's father have passed on a part of yourselves to your baby that will affect his or her life in a predetermined way.

As your body heals from giving birth and your mind heals from the emotional wounds, you will experience a variety of the physical and emotional changes described in the following pages. You may be able to anticipate your reaction if you examine how you have reacted to any losses in the past, such as the death of family members or friends, separations, moves, changes in school, or friends moving away.

Emotional Reactions

You will likely feel a sense of loss and emptiness. You may have difficulty concentrating, or may find yourself becoming forgetful. You will wonder why this is happening to you. You may feel alone, and as if you are the only one facing such an ordeal. Your emotions may make you feel as if you are on a roller coaster. Some days you may feel okay. Other days you may feel down or uptight for no known reason. Grieving has to be emotional because it is difficult to say goodbye. No one ever enjoys separations. It is painful to let your child go without ever knowing if you will see her or him again.

You may feel irritable, moody, restless. You may find yourself feeling dazed and numb, or crying at anything. Tears may come when you least expect them and without previous warning. Crying is okay and is a good way to release pent-up emotions. Do not worry about how much or little you cry. Crying does not measure how much you care. It is only one means of expressing feelings, and crying is not everyone's way. At first you might feel too numb to cry. You might fear that if you break down and express any emotion, you will lose all control. Take everything at your own pace and in your own time.

Crying helps get out sad and angry feelings. The angry feelings can often be a sign of healing. There is energy in anger, and it can help to mobilize you. Feeling the emotions is a positive sign that you are facing your loss rather than denying it. Anger is often behind feelings of depression; some people view depression as anger turned inward toward oneself. Depression paints a picture of lack of energy and helplessness, whereas anger denotes vitality and energy.

You may feel angry at everyone around you for not preventing the loss. It is easier to blame others than to take responsibility for such a serious decision yourself. Or you may feel angry at yourself for letting the pregnancy and adoption happen. Feeling and expressing anger are normal and healthy, but you will need to find nondestructive outlets for these feelings. Unexpressed feelings can result in floods of feelings at unexpected times.

It is important to note that alcohol is a depressant. It can numb you so that your mourning is denied or delayed. Using alcohol to try to cope can be dangerous. It is self-defeating because it does not allow you to fully experience your true feelings. The use of drugs, including sleeping pills or tranquilizers, can also numb you. If you are having severe sleep disturbances, medication might help for a short time to get a good night's rest, but it should be taken with caution and under the care of a physician. Remember that sleep disturbance is a normal reaction following loss.

You may experience an anxiety or panic reaction. You may want to run away and hide. Or you may want to hide inside your house in seclusion forever. Some people have imaginary thoughts after a loss, especially at bedtime. Or you may have nightmares. If you have a history of psychiatric problems, you may be more vulnerable to an intense emotional reaction. Suicidal thoughts are common during an intense grief reaction. You are not going crazy, but if you feel suicidal you should seek professional help right away. Remember that your doctor or mental health specialist is available to help with any emotional problem.

You are going through a period of change and emotional turmoil. This is not a good time to make big decisions or other changes. You will need to maintain as much stability and support as possible during the initial upheaval as you adjust to the loss. Allow yourself some time to heal before making any changes in your life.

Physical Reactions

As well as the expected physical discomfort from delivery, unexpressed feelings may find expression through your body. Feelings that have no outlet will stay hidden inside. They will not go away. Your body and mind are interconnected, inseparable parts of your total being. To have a physical reaction to emotional stress is normal, and it does not mean that the physical reaction is all in your mind.

One clear example of the body's physical response when under emotional pressure is a headache. It can be triggered by muscle tightness and tension brought about through emotional strain. It does not mean that the pain of the headache is any less real than the pain of a bang on the head.

Some of the common physical responses to emotional pain and stress are headaches, bowel problems, sleep disturbances, vomiting, back pain, abdominal pain, aching limbs, increase in or loss of appetite and related weight fluctuations, muscle tension, fatigue, allergic reactions, heart palpitations, dizziness, shortness of breath, or overactivity. It is normal to experience some physical expression of your loss.

Although it is important to recognize the interrelationship of physical symptoms and emotional stress, it is equally important to remember that there might be an underlying medical problem. It is always a good idea to consult with your family doctor if your symptoms persist, before attributing a troublesome symptom to stress.

Postpartum Blues and Depression

Postpartum blues are a normal experience for most women who give birth to a child. In a wanted pregnancy, there is often a low period, with episodes of tearfulness, that occurs a few days following the baby's birth. The mother is facing the reality of becoming a parent and the responsibilities ahead. When you are placing your baby for adoption, it is just as natural to experience postpartum blues as you face the reality for yourself. You will be rebuilding your life again, facing people's reactions and questions, and other adjustments. Postpartum blues may be even greater than usual, because after the hospital stay you have to separate from your baby and say goodbye.

Postpartum depression is different from the more common postpartum blues. It is not just a feeling of being down in the dumps. It can include any or all of the following signs: anxiety, decrease or increase in appetite, guilt feelings, numbness, shame, decrease in sexual drive, nightmares, changes in sleep patterns, feelings of helplessness and hopelessness, or suicidal thoughts or feelings.

If symptoms of depression are present, you should not be making any major decisions, and this includes the decision of adoption. You cannot make an informed, rational decision if you are depressed. Refrain from signing any adoption consents until you consult with a psychiatrist or other professional counselor. It is important to find a professional who understands postpartum depression and takes your concerns seriously. You might feel more comfortable with a female psychiatrist or counselor. Many towns have women's resource or health centers where they can refer you to an expert professional.

Your psychiatrist may prescribe medication such as a tranquilizer or an antidepressant that might help you out of a severe depression or provide temporary relief of symptoms. She or he can also provide support through therapy to help you cope with the loss, which may help to alleviate the depression. This is a time to reach out for the support of family and friends as well as professionals. You need to nurture yourself and let others lend their support.

Your psychiatrist can assess when you are ready to make rational decisions about the adoption option. Your baby can always be placed in foster care for a period of time to allow you to recover from a postpartum depression and rethink your decision. There is no ironclad deadline for you to make your decision; take the time you need.

4
A Time of Transition

Adjustment After the Hospital

One of the most difficult times will be the actual day that you leave the hospital and have to leave your baby behind. The reality of the situation will hit home. At this time you may just want to be alone, but it is an important time to have some people around for support.

Donna: I don't remember how many days I was in the hospital. All I remember of my last day there was getting out of the wheelchair into my mom's car. I try and try to remember if I made a special visit to my son in the nursery before I left, or what my emotional state was, but those memories are locked away.

I moved home to live with my mom and dad again. I hadn't been home many days before I received a call from my social worker. She said that my son had been placed with a wonderful family and that they were very happy to receive such a beautiful baby. I remember that phone call vividly because my mom was nearby, and I didn't want her to see me crying.

About a week or so later, I had my appointment at the adoption agency to sign some papers. I wasn't sure what kind of papers I signed but just knew that they were something to do with the legalities of the adoption. I went by myself to that appointment. My social worker was there and two other people who worked at the agency. I placed my hand on a bible and made all kinds of promises. I repeated out loud everything that I was told to say. The only specific detail that I remember was that I understood that I was giving up all my rights as a natural parent. I signed my name several times to various documents which I didn't read and left the office. When I think of that day, I feel furious. I was just 19 years old, so young and so lost. Why was I alone on that day? Why does the memory remain with me of it being such a cold, heartless experience?

While I was waiting at the bus stop to go home, a fellow whom I had known in school drove by and offered me a lift home. Today, I don't remember who that fellow was, but I do remember our conversation. He said, "So what's new with you?" I replied, "I just gave my baby away." From there we drove home in silence. When I got home I went straight to my room and closed the door. I cried for a very long time.

The time following hospitalization is a major adjustment period. It is a time when support is still very much needed. You will likely have to visit with your social worker to sign the adoption consents a few days following discharge from the hospital. However, once the adoption consents are signed, the adoption issue is not magically over and done with.

Donna: Once my baby was born and the adoption was completed, I had a sense from others that it was now over and finished, as if there was a sigh of relief. But that only made the adjustment more difficult because it wasn't over for me. It was only just beginning, and yet I had to pretend that it was all over and done with. Basically, we all tried to pretend that it never happened. It was only because of my reunion years later that family and friends told me their true feelings.

You will need to give yourself permission to express your feelings. You will need some time to readjust to your routines. You may feel a sense of emptiness or a void.

You will have certain decisions to make about work or school, and goals for yourself. After a major loss of any kind, you are expected to return gradually to your regular life. Keeping active and busy is important, but keeping too busy and overextending yourself into too many areas might make you feel exhausted.

Physical activity can be very healing, but some people feel they lack the necessary energy and concentration. Helping someone else can give you a good feeling. It is important to be kind to yourself. Have a warm bath. Go for a walk. Do something that you really enjoy.

This will be a time for reflection and reorganization. In times of upheaval and change, the need for structure and organization in your life is strong. You may find yourself suddenly housecleaning or reorganizing your world. It may be difficult, though, to get back into your old routines. You may have to find new routines. Remember to keep the changes small and gradual for the time being. All changes require energy and call for adaptation, even changes perceived as positive, such as getting married.

You may have to make decisions regarding your relationship with the baby's father, because he may still be involved in your life. If you still have contact with him, use this opportunity to talk things over. He is a person who can share in your grief, which he may be feeling, too. He could possibly be a significant support for you.

Now that the peak of the crisis is over, you will need to think about birth control to keep all this from happening all over again. As you have found out, it can happen to anyone; just because it has happened to you once does not mean that it cannot happen a second time. Some young women go through a promiscuous stage after relinquishing a child. Some find themselves pregnant a second time. This might mean a second relinquishment, or keeping the baby in an attempt to replace the child lost through relinquishment. Others might decide to marry and quickly have more children to try to replace the lost child and fill the void they feel. Other young women feel that they will never have intercourse again and will thus ensure that an unwanted pregnancy will not occur. However, this unrealistic assumption can lead to a lack of precautions against pregnancy. A new relationship, which you are unprepared for, can take you by surprise and lead to unprotected intercourse and another unwanted pregnancy.

So decisions about birth control are crucial following hospitalization. It is usually recommended that a woman wait at least two weeks following the birth of a child before having intercourse. You should have a follow-up visit to your doctor after your discharge from the hospital. This is an ideal opportunity to discuss birth control methods. There are also family planning clinics such as Planned Parenthood that can be a resource for birth control devices.

There are various methods of birth control such as the birth control pill, the intrauterine device (IUD), the condom, the diaphragm, the cervical cap, and the sponge. It is important to remember that barrier methods such as the condom, the diaphragm, the cervical cap and the sponge are designed to be used along with a jelly or cream that kills sperm. It is most important to find a method that suits your lifestyle so that you will use it consistently and properly.

Birth control is the responsibility of both partners, but it is important for you to ensure protection for yourself because you are the one who would have to go through the unwanted pregnancy. It is now common for women to purchase condoms to keep available in the event of unforeseen intercourse, even though it is a device worn by the male. Communication with your sexual partner is critical and is part of being responsible for your own sexuality, if you intend to prevent a second unplanned pregnancy.

Reactions of Family and Friends

The relationships among family and friends are vital supports during stressful times. However, you will need to let them know how and when you need their support. Family and friends will likely feel uncomfortable talking about the adoption. They will be unsure about how to react. They often do not perceive the aspect of loss in adoption and will not have any guidelines about how to help.

It is a common misconception that the past is behind you and that it is best not to talk about it. Some people may be curious and may ask questions that you are not prepared for. Other people may fear upsetting you by raising the topic. Many people will act as if nothing has happened. This can be very frustrating, because you will feel that so much has happened. You will feel as if you have aged overnight, and yet others around you will not see this.

Your family and friends will mainly take their lead from you. The more comfortable you are in allowing them to talk with you, the more they can reach out to you. If you keep everything a secret, you may lose out on the potential support of those around you. You may find yourself criticized by a person who you thought was a good friend, but you also may find good friends among the least likely individuals. You may be able to predict how family and friends will react, based on how they have reacted to other crises, such as discovering your pregnancy.

You may have a lot of strong feelings against your family and friends because of their reactions to your pregnancy. It is common to blame them for their influence on your adoption decision, or for lack of support. They may not have reacted in the way you had hoped, but remember that they reacted in the only way they knew how at the time. During this period of adjustment after hospitalization, you can begin to talk things out with significant people in your life. It is a time to forgive yourself, your family, and your friends. It is an opportunity to work on understanding each other and repairing relationships. Talking about what has happened is the first crucial step.

> *Donna*: Today mom and dad and I disagree on exactly what transpired. I remember them being really angry and wanting me out of their lives for what I'd done. They remember being very hurt that I had not come to them in the beginning for help. Guilt seems to have a way of disguising the truth. Mom says she could not understand my determination in wanting to give up my child. Yet one of my deciding factors was based on a conversation that I had with mom before my son was born. I understood that my parents didn't want me to keep the child. I suspect it will forever remain a mystery as to who said and felt what. I have often wondered how much of what I remember was contrived in my mind to cover my hurt. In any event, my relationship with my parents was strained during the remaining part of my pregnancy, and the distance between us carried on for many years afterward.

You need to understand that this pregnancy and adoption not only affect you but those close to you, including your family and your boyfriend. They have feelings too, but you may be too preoccupied with your own stress to realize that they are experiencing a crisis alongside you. Your parents and boyfriend will grieve too, often in silence. Your parents grieve for you and for the loss of a grandchild, who may be the first in the family. Your parents and boyfriend may also silently remember the child's birthdays.

Many birthparents look back with regret for not having talked more about the experience with their parents or other birthparents The more time that goes by, the harder it becomes to raise the topic. All the feelings, misunderstandings, and blame may resurface later in life, especially if you decide to pursue reunion. The most positive step that you can take now is to share what you can with those who are important to you. Clear the air now rather than letting hurts and misunderstandings turn into huge rifts in relationships, which can last a lifetime. Talk and cry together. Only then can they be there for you.

Letting Go

The dictionary defines "to let go'" as meaning "to release; to allow to pass without comment; to talk at length especially when angry." The words "to let" mean "to allow and to give permission." So this section on letting go is about allowing yourself to release self-destructive feelings that punish and hurt you. These feelings and the behaviors they connect with keep you stuck in life and block you from moving forward. You can feel selfish, guilty, unmotherly, uncaring, unloving, or unlovable. The behavior can include alcohol abuse, drug abuse, eating disorders, or suicide attempts. Or you may be stuck in cycles of self-blame or blame of others. You might be preoccupied with thoughts about your baby and the loss you experienced.

Gradually releasing these feelings helps to break these self-defeating cycles. One way is to begin to tell your feelings to someone else such as a friend, family member, counselor, or another birthparent. You are entitled to have these feelings, but they should not be allowed to control your life. You need to be in charge of your life, and you have choices about where you expend your energy. Self-blame and blame of others take a tremendous amount of energy that could be channeled into your growth and happiness.

You have paid your dues. Yes, you placed a baby for adoption, and it may be unpleasant to know that you made this decision, but you are not mean, uncaring, unmotherly, unnatural, cruel, or unloving. You are a human being who is feeling hurt. To continue to punish yourself will not change the circumstances that led to your decision, and will not change the decision. You acted in the best way you knew how in view of the circumstances at the time.

You deserve to go on with your life and find happiness and satisfaction. You are allowed to feel good. But first you will have to forgive yourself. It is only human to make mistakes in life. If this were your daughter or another birthparent or friend going through the same experience, would you forgive them? If so, then why do you judge yourself so harshly?

Letting go of the self-punishment and self-blame will not mean that you are being disloyal to your child. You do not have to punish yourself for your baby's sake. No one will be helped by your self-destructive feelings, least of all you. You do not have to choose the role of a victim. This is your opportunity to recognize any mistakes you have made. The crisis has placed you at a transition point. It is a time for reevaluation and new beginnings.

Can Pain Be Positive?

Unfortunately, growth and learning can often follow experiences that shake us up. Although it may seem that the pain that often comes is futile, you will learn and grow, and increase your sensitivity to other troubled individuals. You have learned many things from this experience that cannot be learned from any type of book or school. This loss will sensitize you to others' troubles. Many people turn to a career in the helping professions after a personal crisis. If you are considering this for your future, it is of utmost importance that you work through your grief and personal issues so that you can be objective when helping others. Otherwise your own personal experience can cloud your judgment and be a hindrance rather than a help to others. You must feel in control of your life before you can help others sort out their problems.

You have learned how to cope with a very difficult and stressful situation. You have learned to make difficult decisions. The same strengths you found within yourself to cope with this experience will be the strengths that will help you cope with life's other events, adjustments, and crises. Life is never without its downs as well as ups, and you will use these strengths again at some point in the future. You have become a stronger person from all that you have endured.

> *Sue*: I learned to feel a lot stronger. I've always said that if I had to face other painful decisions in life, it could never be as hard as giving up my daughter for adoption. I've also learned to be more flexible and open-minded regarding values and life. I guess I grew up in a hurry, although I was an adult at the time.

Self-Esteem: Looking After Yourself

A strong sense of self-worth and self-determination are two of the basic ingredients that help anyone cope with crises. Self-esteem means having a positive opinion of yourself—that you are a worthwhile and valuable individual. You cannot expect others to respect you and treat you well if you do not respect yourself. It also means accepting yourself—your strengths and weaknesses. No one is perfect. Self-blame decreases self-esteem.

Many birthparents feel unworthy, unloving, and different. If you feel down on yourself, you will be more sensitive to the comments of others, and you might misinterpret others' opinions as criticism. You might misconstrue situations, so it is important to keep your communication lines open.

Similarly, the stronger you feel inside, the less you worry about what other people think. Self-esteem is the most precious gift you can give yourself. Most of all, you have to be good to yourself. If you think poorly of yourself, then you will choose friends or a spouse who will treat you with the same disregard. It is a two-way process. If you want to give to others and expect nurturing in return, you must first nurture yourself. Otherwise you will have nothing to give and therefore nothing to get back.

Allow yourself time with people who make you feel good. Stay away from those who bring you down, or make you feel ashamed or uncomfortable. You have control over whom you associate with. Even one good friend can be invaluable. It can be hard to reach out for support when you are in distress and feeling vulnerable, but it can be so comforting. If you isolate yourself from people, you will deny yourself the possibility of that comfort. Most people find that support and nurturing come from one or two close relationships. If you do not have any close friends or family to turn to, meeting with others in similar situations or finding an understanding counselor could be the support you need.

Born Twice

You touched me with your smile
I stayed with you awhile
But as I know
You had to go
Through life we both must learn
  I'd wandered many a road
  And many a spirit glowed
  I wanted you
  To live anew
  To share a family's love

I hope your heart is free
You've grown away from me
You're on my mind
Another time
The pain will pass away
　　And now I've paid the price
　　You've really been born twice:
　　Once with me
　　The other—free
　　Into a world of care
Another life has been
Where I could not have seen
She watched you grow
But this I know
We live in unity

—Imelda Buckley

5
Looking Back on the Adoption Decision

Often, even years after the decision for adoption, you may have many unresolved feelings such as regret, anger or blame. You may say to yourself, "If only I had...."— especially if you felt pressured into a decision at the time. It is never too late to work on these unresolved feelings, even if decades have elapsed. This section of the book will lead you back in time to help you rethink matters from a new perspective. This means looking at the past honestly and without blaming yourself or others.

Reconstructing Past Circumstances

If the relinquishment has already occurred, and it may have been many years ago, it can help to look back at your circumstances at the time. Think back to the time when you found that you were pregnant. Most likely you were either a teenager or young adult living at home and dependent on your parents, or recently living on your own. You were probably naive and not assertive with people in authority because you were still learning how to cope in adulthood. You were likely still struggling with growing-up tasks such as independence, identity, peer relationships, career goals, and sexuality.

Your baby may have been the result of your first love. Or you may have been experimenting with newfound sexuality. It might have been an uncomfortable sexual encounter that brings back painful memories.

Remember back to the intensity of the feelings you experienced at the time. What did it feel like? You were probably in a state of emotional turmoil, possibly facing the first major crisis in your life. You would likely have felt overwhelmed with out-of-control emotions. It would be unusual to look back and feel no pain or have no regrets at all.

Whatever your experience, you did not have the perspective that you have now. It may appear that you could have done something quite differently, but you need to be realistic because you know now what you could not know then. You could not foresee the future.

You might feel that you could have handled keeping your baby, but if you chose to keep your baby back then, your life could have taken a different course. You might not be in the same position that you are in now. Maybe it would have been easier than you had envisioned at the time if supports had been offered, but maybe it would have been harder. The fact is that you will never know, and it is impossible to speculate on what might have been. Rehashing it in your mind is self-punishment.

One birthparent provided this description of reconstruction : "It is like cleaning out your drawers. First you take out the crumpled clothes and sort through them one by one. You put them in order and place them back neatly in the drawer." It is this new sense of order and control that you need to strive for.

Your Choice

As you reconstruct the circumstances and feelings, you will need to reexamine your decision to choose adoption. Why did you choose this option over keeping your baby or having an abortion? Carefully assess everything you considered in arriving at this decision. Did you feel free to make the decision on your own, or did you feel pressured or influenced by others? Did you secretly wish someone else would make the decision for you or would tell you what was best? Did you feel you even had a choice?

Whatever your reason, it was a valid one. It had to be made with your interests in mind as well as the baby's, or it would not have been sound. If you made the decision just for your baby without taking yourself into consideration, you may be left with many regrets. Also, if you made the decision to please your parents or under pressure from a social worker, doctor, or well-meaning individual, you may be left with anger.

Even though you may not have felt there was a choice, because of tremendous pressure from others, it was you who signed the consents. An action made under duress can be very difficult to accept. Nonetheless, you took a passive role in the decision-making process. It is not surprising, however, that you gave into pressure. You are only human. You may be left feeling angry with the others, but if you continue to dwell on the pressure from others, you will continue to feel helpless in your everyday life.

The more freedom you felt to make your own decision, the easier it is to accept your decision without blame and regret looming in the background. Regardless of the way the decision took place, it was not easy, because there is no easy answer for a pregnant teenager or young adult. Give yourself credit for not having made a quick, irrational decision. No one takes an adoption decision lightly.

Guilt and Anger

Guilt is defined in the dictionary as meaning, "state of having offended; sinful; wicked; judged to have committed a crime." Some birthparents feel as if they have committed a crime. Some feel they should be punished for making such an unmotherly decision. Some feel judged by society for having done something terribly unnatural and wrong. It is sad that so many caring, capable women are left with such terrible feelings about themselves. They have not committed crimes. Birthparents have only made decisions based upon an acceptable option within society. In fact, today's society is trying to entice more pregnant teenagers to choose adoption over other options in unwanted pregnancy. Still, many birthparents retain the feeling that they did something wicked and unmotherly.

> *Sue*: The feeling of guilt was very strong for at least a year. I dealt with it by moving away from the area. I ended up in another country and moved around for years.

Ironically, it is the element of choice that adds to the feelings of guilt. In other kinds of loss, the person tends to move past the guilt once they recognize that they could not have prevented the loss. Birthmothers however, made a choice and consequently are left feeling responsible for it. This leaves many birthmothers with tremendous guilt, often for years to come if it remains unexpressed. Some birthmothers blame others in an effort to reduce feelings of guilt.

> *Pauline*: I continue to question my decision about giving my baby up for adoption. A part of me knows that I had no other option, but another part of me says that I do not

know if he's in a good home. Maybe he would have been better off with me.

If your feelings of guilt remain unresolved, then you must be assuming that a wrong has been committed and that a punishment is due. Consciously or unconsciously you may seek punishment for yourself. You may then enter relationships with persons who will fulfill this view of yourself, or you may punish yourself through self-destructive behavior. Sometimes teenagers act out their feelings in unruly behavior to attract punishment. But in adoption the punishment can never fit the crime, because no crime has been committed. Guilt is the feeling most in need of reevaluation. Is the degree of guilt that you are carrying realistic? It will not bring your baby back. Continuing to punish yourself will not help.

Pauline: The guilt and other painful emotions that I experienced during my pregnancy and the loss of my child have eroded my self-esteem. My marriage and other relationships have all been affected. I don't feel like a worthwhile person who deserves love and caring.

Behind the guilt is often unexpressed anger. Anger is a normal reaction to any loss. Unexpressed anger can turn inward against yourself and bring depression, added guilt, and self-punishment.

Many people fear expressing anger because it is not viewed as socially acceptable. Some fear losing control of pent-up emotions. So it is important to work on anger gradually and seek professional help if you feel intense rage inside. When anger is released, the energy can then be channeled in a positive direction. Some birthparents direct their anger toward making changes in the adoption system.

Your anger may have been justified initially, but it is not helping you if you hang onto it for years. It is necessary to get the anger and guilt behind you by getting these feelings off your chest. It is never too late to make peace with yourself.

6
Issues in Adulthood:
Living with Your Decision

After the period of acute grief has passed, you will begin your readjustment back into the mainstream of life. This whole experience will have an impact on various elements of your adult life including future decisions, relationships, and your opinion of yourself. It will leave some areas that will remain sensitive for a lifetime.

> *Donna*: As they say, life goes on. I eventually got a job and moved into an apartment with a friend. I've had several jobs, several different apartments, and many friends. I've never married, although I've had committed relationships. I lead a fairly simple life. The single thread that remained throughout is my feeling about my son. I have thought about him every single day for the last 16 years. We had such a short time together, but my love for him has remained constant if not stronger as time goes by.
>
> I kept a mental record of his progress by imagining what he was doing and was interested in, by comparing him with other children his age. I imagined his first birthday party, his first day in school, and his first bicycle. I've seen children romping in playgrounds and have thought to myself, "Maybe that's him kicking a soccer ball." When I saw a sick or handicapped child, I prayed that my son was not handicapped.
>
> I have a young cousin who is the same age as my son. I would always ask about his interests, especially as he got into his teenage years. My cousin's bedroom was covered with posters of rock stars, and I would imagine my son's room to be the same. Relating to other children was the only means that I had of keeping in touch with my son. Many times I would worry or be afraid for him. What if he was unhappy or mistreated? Did he know why I chose to have him adopted, and why I couldn't see him again? Did

he know that I cared? Did he love me or hate me? As each year went by my wanting to know more about him got stronger. I began to feel that as he got older, he had every right to know more about his heritage. I assumed that he and his adoptive family knew as little about myself and my family as I knew about him.

Sensitive Areas

You will continue to remember and have feelings about your child while most others around you will forget. Your emotions will vary in intensity depending on what triggers them and on the degree to which you have worked through your grief.

The following are some common sensitive areas for birthparents:

- Child's birthday

- Special songs that remind you of the pregnancy and child

- TV, radio shows, books, or newspaper articles about adoption, pregnancy, or loss

- Pregnancies of friends, coworkers, or relatives

- Others discussing pregnancy, birth, adoption, or children

- Being around babies or children

- Baby showers

- Visiting a new mother in the hospital

- Meeting a child of the same age as yours or with the same name

- The birth of the next child in your extended family

- Making decisions about having future children

- Making decisions in other areas of your life, especially those that involve possibilities of loss or separation (for example, marriage)

- Future pregnancies and deliveries
- Sexuality
- Other losses
- Family events or special occasions

Pauline: I find that, since the birth of my baby, being around friends and relatives' babies or their pregnancies is very painful. I find myself wondering what my child was like at a similar age, and whether there is a family resemblance.

On special days that bring strong reminders of your child, such as birthdays or Christmas, you can find your own way of marking the occasion. You might buy some flowers for your home, play a special song, or mark the occasion in some way that is significant to you. Even though your child is not physically part of your life, he or she will live in your memory, and it is okay to remember your child in your own way.

You may find the language of adoption uncomfortable, as in reference to yourself as a birthmother or birthfather. There are no clear words to describe your relationship to your offspring, and this can make conversations confusing and awkward.

It is also hard to sort out how to refer to your child. It may be difficult to actually say your child's name aloud because you have not had the opportunity to do so, to desensitize yourself to what it sounds like. Even saying the name can evoke tremendous emotion.

The following are some of the most difficult questions or statements to deal with:

- Do you have any children?
- You don't have any children so how would you know?
- Are you going to have children?
- Why don't you have any children?
- Don't you like children?
- Don't you want to have any children?
- You'll know what its like when you have children of your own.

- How many children do you have?

- You can't imagine what being separated from one's child is like!

- Don't you just love babies!

- I don't know how anyone could give her own baby away!

Other talk that is bound to evoke emotional, awkward reactions include comments of others when you are having your next child. They assume it is your first child and offer all kinds of advice about pregnancy and delivery, and you may want to yell out that this is not your first child!

Many situations will make you react emotionally. You may find yourself immobilized or speechless. Afterwards you will think of all the things you wished you had said. It is natural that you will feel sensitive and be caught off guard at times with comments or questions. The other person will not realize that these are emotionally laden topics. You will have to make decisions throughout your life when these topics arise as to how much or how little you want to say about your experience. Each time you talk about your experience it will get easier, but there will always be some situations that will be particularly uncomfortable.

Holding on to Memories

Memories are almost all that you have to validate that your experience actually happened and that your baby existed. Some people are fortunate enough to have mementos to remind them of the child.

The fewer concrete mementos that you have, the more you will need to cling to memories to avoid forgetting, and the more you may try to keep the memories as fresh and vivid as possible. Thinking about the situation uses a great deal of energy and is emotionally draining.

Memories can fade and become distorted over time. Writing them down helps to retain the details. You do not have to keep recalling the memory to ensure the details are not forgotten. Because of the components of secrecy and shame, many women have kept all the information in their heads, and as a result, have

forgotten important facts. Some birthmothers forget such significant details as the date of the child's birth. This leaves them feeling
upset or guilty. Memory gaps are common because your defenses
were so strong that they could have kept you in the numb stage to
avoid feeling pain. It is important to piece together any information
you can gather, no matter how small.

Other members of your family may also have their special
memories and sensitive areas. Your parents may wish that they
could find out more about their grandchild. They may remember
the grandchild's birthday with sadness. They may not tell you of
their feelings, and you may assume that they do not care or
remember. It may surprise you to find out the extent of their
feelings if you make the effort to talk about it later in life.

Keeping or Revealing the Secret

When an event is kept secret it implies that it is something to
be ashamed of and hidden. If you continue to keep the secret, you
are buying into this view. It will be difficult to feel good about
yourself if you must keep a significant part of your past hidden for
fear of being judged by others, but disclosing your secret is painful.

> *Pauline*: I ask myself now, "How did I manage to keep this
> painful secret for so long?" I blocked it out as if it just
> didn't happen. However, when family or friends had a
> discussion about babies or pregnancy, my secret wasn't as
> deeply buried as I thought. My pain would start to sur-
> face, and I would have to leave.

Gradually letting go of the secret is a release from the bondage
of shame and embarrassment; you will feel a sense of relief. It can
actually build your confidence as you find the courage to talk about
this part of your life. There are few natural openings in everyday
conversations that allow you to talk about your relinquishment
experience. You will have to look for opportunities. You may be
most comfortable beginning to talk with other women who have
placed babies for adoption. You will need to gain confidence by
sharing first with people who will be supportive and nonjudgmen-
tal, unlike people around you who may not understand and may
warn you to leave the past alone.

The less secrecy there is from the beginning, the less you will have to reveal later in life, but you will always be meeting new persons who are unaware of this part of your past. You will have to decide whom, when, and how to tell. Most birthparents share their experience with boyfriends, spouses, and eventually with their future children. Sometimes other children see your sensitivity to adoption issues and fear that they are adopted. Even birthfathers usually tell their spouses of the baby who was placed for adoption.

The fear that many birthparents have that their children will think badly of them is rarely justified. Children tend to be curious about their half-siblings and may encourage you toward search and reunion. Discussing the adoption with those close to you can give you an opportunity to enrich relationships.

Throughout life you will have to decide how you will respond to awkward questions about how many children you have. You will have to weigh why the question is being posed, by whom, the time and place, and the possible reactions. If you feel comfortable with the question, you can use it as an opportunity to talk about the adoption and begin the process of release. You may feel like running and hiding when such questions are asked, but dealing directly with them can make you feel proud of yourself.

If you are planning to search for your child or file with a reunion registry in the future, disclosing the facts with those around you leaves less explaining to do later on if a reunion takes place. There will be a continual process of explaining this new relationship to a variety of people who come into your life. Each time you tell someone, it makes the next time a little easier.

> *Sue*: When I moved away after the birth, the "secret" was not a problem. I did not return to my homeland for almost six years. This secret has reared its head again as my search begins because there are people I must confide in.

As you talk about your adoption experience with others, you may be surprised at the number of people who are linked in some way to adoption. It is comforting to find other people to talk to who understand the sensitive nature of adoption issues.

Having Other Children

Whether to have subsequent children can be a sensitive and complicated question. Some birthmothers remain single. Some choose not to have other children because it might be too distressing. Others feel that having more children would somehow be disloyal to the child who was placed for adoption. Some seek to be sure that the next child is wanted, and born in a supportive situation in contrast to the crisis surrounding the first pregnancy.

Others might get pregnant soon after the relinquishment as a way of replacing the lost baby. Unfortunately, a second child cannot replace the first, and a second crisis may be precipitated. Some people keep the second baby to prove something to themselves or others. Others surrender the second child to try to reassure themselves that adoption was in fact the best course of action. The reasons for an immediate second pregnancy are complex, but one must be alert to the fact that behavior can be the result of subconscious needs that are not obvious or easily understood.

Some birthmothers find themselves unable to have subsequent children, and may be faced with the difficult question of adopting a child. The inability may seem like punishment for the relinquishment, and you may feel cheated, angry, or resentful. It is extremely important to have resolved within yourself the aftermath of the relinquishment so that anger is not displaced onto an adopted child. A birthparent who adopts a child is taking on two quite different roles, those of birthparent and adoptive parent, that must somehow be integrated.

If you do have more children, it is important not to name any after the first one. Each child is unique and deserves his or her own name. You may place expectations on a child to somehow make up for the one you lost through adoption.

Future pregnancies are bound to bring back emotions related to the earlier pregnancy. You can anticipate that you will relive some of the past events; if your grief was buried, it could easily surface.

Some birthparents fear losing subsequent children and feel their parenting style is overprotective. You may feel a need to prove to yourself that you can be a good parent. Separation from subsequent children may be an issue.

7
Issues for Others in the Adoption Triangle

Adoption is a lifelong process for all involved; it does not end when the adoption is legalized. Those involved are all subject to generalizations, stereotypes, and myths. It is important for every party involved to be sensitive to the others' feelings, needs, positions, and roles.

Adoptive Parents

Adoptive parents represent a cross-section of society just as all other members of the adoption triangle do. Adoptive families have their problems, stresses, even divorces, as in other families, and they have to deal with additional issues and demands that adoption brings. Adoptive parenthood is a lifelong experience.

If you are a birthparent and have never met an adoptive parent, you should try to do so. It can be an enlightening experience. It is common for birthparents to have fears, strong feelings, and misconceptions about adoptive parents. Some birthparents feel grateful to the adoptive parents; others feel resentful that the adoptive parents were in a position to take care of the child and reaped the joys of parenthood. Birthparents' feelings often depend on the degree of choice they felt in placing the baby for adoption in the first place. The more comfortable and in control of the decision they felt, the more comfortable they are able to feel.

The experience of loss links all members in the adoption triangle. Loss of fertility was the major loss adoptive parents had to face. Just as in other losses there is a grief reaction, and acceptance needs to take place. They must deal with the realization that there will be no biological children from the marriage. This loss hits at the core of peoples' self-worth and is not an easy adjustment to make, having involved extensive fertility tests, medical interventions, and disappointments. At the present time, infertility is the principal reason for adoption.

Telling children they were adopted should be a gradual process as their capacity to understand develops. This means that the adoptive parents have to deal with their infertility many times again. It is an emotional experience each time, and hard for adoptive parents to find the right way to explain how adoption happens. Many birthparents wonder and worry about what the adoptive parents have told the child about them, often fearing that they have been painted in a negative light to the child. The various kinds of open adoption that are being experimented with, as discussed earlier in this book, arise partly to diminish unknowns.

Progress is being made in educating adoptive parents and applicants for adoption about the realities of adoption, such as avoiding pretending that the child is their biological child. Adoptive parents themselves have also formed support groups to help them understand adoption issues, and have joined together in large associations to educate the public and improve services.

Adoptees

It is the adopted children who have the central role in the adoption triangle. Both sets of parents are connected through their relationship to the children, who are the only persons clearly not party to the decision about their own life's path. Adopted children, growing into adults, were the main force in bringing about changes in adoption legislation through the formation of activist groups. Many adoptees resent the secrecy and confidentiality surrounding their own birth information, and continue to lobby for access to their birth records. Some adoptees feel that their identity is not complete as a result of being denied such essential information.

When adoptees conduct a search, they are looking for their roots and genealogy. They want specific information about their history to help them feel complete. Roots and history are important to many people, and many nonadopted people discover their roots by researching their family genealogy. For adoptees who have no background details, it can become even more significant. But it is not important to all adoptees, just as it is not important to everyone in society.

Biological families naturally sort out who resembles whom in looks and personality. If there is no one similar in the immediate nuclear family, the person usually finds a connection with an extended family member: "Your red hair came from Aunt Mary."

This connecting with the past is part of the formation of identity. It is missing for adoptees.

When adoptees search for birthparents, they are not searching for a "mommy and daddy." They are looking for a link with their biological family. They want to know whom they look like. Having their own children often evokes adoptees' desire to know more about birthparents, both because they are faced with this identity gap in their history, and because they became more conscious of the genetic physical and medical characteristics their children will be inheriting.

Adoptees differ, however, in their level of desire to discover their past. It is known that more females search than males, and the reasons for this are unclear. It may have to do with the role that females often take in terms of keeping families emotionally connected, or with the maternal childbearing role.

Adoptees have especially sensitive issues to face concerning identity, separation, and abandonment, although the degree to which adopted children and adults have difficulty coping with these issues varies. One myth about adoptees is that only those who are unhappy in their adoptive homes search for birthparents. This is incorrect. If adoptees have had an unhappy homelife, however, it may affect their expectations in a reunion with birthparents. They may desire more than the birthparents are willing or able to give. The birthparents cannot make up for the past, but can help adoptees in discovering their history.

Birthfathers

Birthfathers are often the most forgotten party in adoption. For this reason, throughout this book, the word birthparent rather than birthmother is used to denote that both birthparents have feelings about the decision and the loss. Birthfathers have also had to face a crisis as teenagers or young adults. They have been the last participants in the adoption process to begin coming out of the closet. Gradually they are speaking up and being recognized as having an important role. This may be a reflection of the shift in North American society to place increased importance on fathering.

Birthfathers have rarely been allowed involvement in the decision-making process. Some birthmothers would have liked the support of birthfathers but were met with rejection, but sometimes birthfathers were never even told about the pregnancy. Studies show that in the majority of situations, however, the birthfathers and birthmothers had a significant relationship with each other. Even as adults they usually know the whereabouts of the other partner. When efforts have been made to involve birthfathers, many have participated in counseling and decision making. Birthfathers have been unfairly stereotyped as being uncaring and uninvolved. They may also feel concerned and upset by the whole ordeal and may feel a sense of responsibility, while feeling helpless to improve the situation.

Males often have an even more difficult time expressing emotions than females, and so the grief process can be very difficult for them. Society is only just beginning to recognize that birthmothers grieve following adoption, and people are even less likely to see the hurt that birthfathers feel. Consequently, supports will be even less available. Fathers form attachments to babies too. Birthfathers' feelings should be recognized not just by society and adoption agencies, but by birthmothers.

> *Sue*: At the first news of my pregnancy, the father was positive. We were going to get married, which is something we had talked of before. Then he was away for six months. I guess I got cold feet. But his letters were full of love and concern, which was really important. We lost contact for some years. Then I moved back to the same province and looked him up when I was in the area on business. Finally a few years later, I talked to him about it and found that he had questions. He had often wondered about our daughter. He agreed to have his name on a reunion registry and would be there for our daughter if she wished to know us. It was a wonderful feeling to discuss our daughter and know he loves her too.

Birthfathers may not agree with the adoption decision and may feel totally powerless to intervene. They are often blamed by both sets of (grand) parents as being responsible for the pregnancy. Birthfathers also keep the birth and adoption secret. They usually tell their future spouse but seldom anyone else. They often have even less opportunity than birthmothers to see the baby or express feelings of grief. They may go through life for many years with unresolved feelings and with no adequate understanding of the basis for these feelings; they may find feelings reactivated when basis for these feelings; they may find feelings reactivated when they later have children, and might make the connection at that time. Remember that most of the issues discussed in this book pertain to birthfathers as well as birthmothers.

Adoption policies are gradually changing to acknowledge birthfathers' rights. Now agencies often have to make a reasonable effort to obtain the consent of the father. If birthfathers are encouraged by the adoption system to take a more active role, they may be more available to birthmothers for support. Birthmothers often have unresolved feelings about their child's father. Consulting with the fathers during the decision making may improve communication and decrease secrecy later, should reunion occur. One hopes this would result in the adoptees being encouraged to meet birthfathers as well as birthmothers.

Adoption records would be more accurate if information were obtained directly from birthfathers. Some birthmothers give inaccurate information about the fathers, for a variety of reasons. Or they simply may not have much information about them. Birthmothers may not realize that any false information they have supplied could be passed on to the adoptee. It is unfortunate that some adoptees go through life with an inaccurate impression of their parentage because the mother did not think through the repercussions of supplying misleading information.

8
REUNION

The Adoption Cover-Up

I must know where I'm from, I must know who I am
Someone a part of me exists in this country, free
Records closed, unavailable—hard to get, so incredible
If this country is free, then WHY must this be?
    We are the ones to very dearly pay
    The price of being given up on that day
    We are "The Chosen Ones," that's what they say
    There's no hope for us, not even a ray.
We must "Be grateful" but somehow I can't
In my mind reverberates the chant,
"I must know, I must find my identity, too;
I have the right as the nonadopted do."
    Both parents took their rights with the decision once made
    My life now forgotten as theirs start to fade
    The decision now final, not mine to revoke
    Hidden in obscurity by those who spoke.
As adults, our right to search has been stolen
Our lives are on hold, the web has been woven
The deceit and the lies, "Held in Confidence," they say
The frustration, the price the adoptee must pay.
    Our heritage taken, our identity snuffed
    Our efforts to resolve are always rebuffed
    Everyone else is considered but us
    So we are in limbo amid all their fuss.
As we pay this price, the government gloats
They think they've the power our lives to reproach
Our experiences worthless, reputed to be
The callous our struggle unwilling to see.
        —Adoptee Jennifer Bige (September 5, 1988)

Search

The decision to search for your child is highly personal and individual. Many birthparents have extensive fantasies about search and reunion, but not everyone searches. Some birthparents wait and hope that their children will seek them out once they reach adulthood, and the birthparents may register with a reunion registry. They may not necessarily conduct a search of their own. Some birthparents do not want to interfere with the child's life. Some think that the child might live in an affluent home and might be ashamed of them. Other concerns include fear of rejection, of finding an abused or ill child, or of uncovering a horrible situation. And there is a small number of birthparents who want nothing to do with their offspring.

Whatever the feelings, fears, and fantasies, you must decide for yourself whether to initiate a search for your child. There are no guarantees that you will not find a tragic situation. If you initiate a search, you must be prepared for all the eventualities. Reunion brings reality, not a romantic fantasy.

First of all, you must think through your reason for the search. Keep in mind that searching is a normal reaction to loss, not a way to grieve. Work through your grief as much as you can before considering a search, because engaging in a search is an emotional ordeal that may revive unresolved issues. Some birthparents hold in their grief, hoping that someday they will be reunited with their children and then all will be okay. This usually leads to disaster because all the feelings of grief will surface at a time that in itself is a tremendous emotional upheaval for everyone involved.

Some birthparents believe that if they find their children, they will stop hurting. Searching, however, will not take away the feelings of loss. Your baby is no longer a baby or even a child anymore. You cannot go back in time to recapture a mother-child relationship. You cannot walk into your child's life expecting to be his or her "real" mother. Your child has a mother, father, and family who have raised him, so do not expect to be a rescuer for your child. It could turn out that your child has not had a good upbringing in his adoptive family, but you cannot go back in time and undo what has occurred. The more realistic your expectations are, the more chance you have of building a relationship with your child, if you do meet.

Searching, though, does not necessarily mean meeting your child. You may search for information about your child's situation. Some birthparents do gather some preliminary information and then stop because it is complicated, time-consuming, and emotionally exhausting to continue. You can begin gathering nonidentifying information from the adoption agency and hospital records. This in itself may fill in some gaps, recall events, and validate the experience. Reunion registries are another option, once your child has reached adulthood, and this will be discussed later.

More commonly, adult adoptees initiate a search for their birthparents. This usually means locating the birthmother first and then reaching the father through information obtained from the birthmother. If a reunion occurs on an adoptee's initiative, a birthmother who had not begun a search might not be emotionally prepared. Once again, it is important to work through your feelings and to anticipate all eventualities to avoid being taken off guard.

Of course, you cannot fully prepare yourself for an event that may never take place. If it does occur, you may not have much warning. This is one reason for being as open as possible over the years with significant people in your life, so that you have their support and understanding if you are unexpectedly reunited with your child. If reunion does happen, it will affect the lives of all those around you, as well as your own.

Searching for a birthchild is still a controversial issue in society and is not totally accepted as a wise venture. You will need the support of many people, but you may find that family and friends are not as supportive as you might have anticipated, and they might not really understand your needs. They may feel that you are opening a can of worms, especially if you are initiating the search. Many other well-meaning individuals will give you advice on what to do and how to handle the search and reunion, but it is a highly personal matter, and you must be prepared to sift through the advice and take control of your own search and reunion process. Proceed at your own pace and according to your own needs. You have waited a long time for this reunion. Take time to plan. It will be well worth the effort. Proceed slowly. Be sure you have adequate emotional support. Reevaluate your motivations and expectations and keep them realistic.

The Reunion Itself

> *Donna*: My suggestion for others entering a reunion is to take it slowly. Two months passed after my initial contact before I met my son. That gave us time to think, calm down, and put things in perspective.

You can begin with phone contact, writing letters, and exchanging pictures to gradually get to know one another, preparing for the face-to-face contact. Dropping in on anyone unexpectedly is setting yourself up for disaster. You are only one of the parties in the reunion. Your child is now an adult and may have his or her own needs and ideas about how the reunion might be arranged. It may not fit your fantasy, because it will be reality with the feelings of many people to take into consideration.

Arrangements for the actual face-to-face reunion vary, and should be planned cooperatively. Some find it helpful to meet in a neutral place such as a cafe or park. It is a good idea to bring some pictures along with you. The meeting will feel very intense, so it can be better to have a series of brief contacts rather than one marathon visit. If you have to travel to another city, it is much better to stay in a hotel than to try staying at your son's or daughter's own home, which could be too overwhelming for either to handle. Most people want the first meeting to be private, without the presence of others such as adoptive parents or an intermediary.

Support from a search organization can be of great benefit both practically and emotionally. It helps to talk with people who have conducted searches and had reunions. It is still relatively new, and there are no set rules. It is an opportunity to learn from the experiences of others. Informative booklets are available from Concerned United Birthparents.

> *Pauline*: At a certain age, I realized that I would not be having any more children. I joined a support group for people in the adoption triangle. My child is not old enough yet to register in the reunion registry, but I am planning on advertising and registering as soon as he is of legal age. At this time, I am searching, scared and excited about what could happen in the next year or two.

Aftermath

Having a reunion means facing whatever reality lies ahead, with all possibilities open. That you are related by birth does not mean that you will have an instant relationship. Relationships take time, honesty, and hard work.

There are many decisions to be made as the reunion proceeds.

The adoptee may want to meet other family members. You are not the only important person in his or her biological family tree. The birthmother is usually the key to locating other relatives, and if you have kept the birth and adoption of your child secret, you will have to consider opening up these secrets, now and in the future, if the adoptee seeks extended family contacts.

> *Donna:* The secrecy never goes away. Even though all my family and most of my friends know about my son, it is still treated as a secret. The issue is not comfortably or commonly discussed. I'm unsure if it is the way that I present the topic or if it is others' degree of discomfort.

If you maintain a shroud of secrecy and continue contact with the adoptee without honesty about the relationship, such as introducing him or her to others as a friend, the lack of honesty will interfere with the relationship over time. This also holds true for an adoptee who cannot be honest about his or her relationship to you and insists on introducing you as a friend or distant relative.

You will also have to get used to referring to your child by the name given her or him by the adoptive parents. You have likely thought of your child over the years by the name you gave at birth. Most likely, however, the only name he or she has known was that given by the adoptive parents.

The adoptee will likely want to meet the birthfather. If you are unwilling to provide information about the birthfather to the adoptee, this can be a major block in the potential for your relationship. The birthfather is just as much part of the adoptee's biological heritage as you are, and you will have to decide how to handle the inevitable questions about the birthfather, if you want a rewarding relationship with your offspring.

You will also have to consider whether you will meet the adoptive parents. Remember that no one owns adoptees. They have two sets of parents who have different functions and impacts on them. They will remain connected to both sets of parents throughout life. The attitudes and feelings of the adoptive parents must be taken into consideration, because a reunion affects all three parties in the adoption triangle. The significance of the adoptive parents in the lives of adoptees cannot be discounted. Your respect for this relationship is essential if you are to truly appreciate your son's or daughter's feelings and needs.

Sometimes spouses, children, and significant others in your life may feel displaced by this special attention to another relationship. You will have to consider the feelings of those around you when you become preoccupied, overexcited, or overwhelmed with the reunion experience. You will need these support persons more than ever to help you through this emotional time, so do not take them for granted or overlook the intensity of their reaction to your situation.

A rejection may well be the hardest of the possible outcomes to deal with, but it can happen. Not all adoptees want to meet their birthparents. They, too, have had to cope with their separation from their birthparents and have coped in their own way. Not facing you may be a part of it, or they may feel content with their life as it is, but you can really feel hurt. Remember, however, that rejection does not mean personal rejection because the adoptee does not even know you, or all the facts concerning the relinquishment. These adoptees may not need to get to know their birthparents at this time or at any point in the future. Many birthparents say that they just want to know that their child is okay and that their main concern is for the child. You may be put to the ultimate test of this if your child does not want to meet you, or does meet you and does not wish a relationship. Can you truly put his or her needs first and accept this reality?

You will have to incorporate the reunion experience into your life as a whole. It is one event and one more relationship to sort out and put in perspective. You will have to make certain decisions, such as what you will call each other, how you view the relationship to each other, and how often to see each other. You will both have to reexamine your expectations of the relationship. The main task will be communicating and building a relationship based on these mutual, realistic expectations.

> *Donna*: It has been two years now since my son and I were reunited. Although everything is going well, I still feel that it takes care and planning to ensure that the relationship will continue to go well. I take nothing for granted. Sometimes I am afraid that something will go wrong, and I'll lose my son again. I learned to deal with reunion with each step that I took, and I'm still learning. There are no rules other than those that you have in your heart.

Only a Love Song

I know there is a reason
That we have been growing apart
But choosing to love you forever
I've chosen for growth in my heart
> *This is only a love song, my daughter*
> *If it be as it is now*
> *That you must be hidden from view*
> *I pray that these loving strains*
> *Find a way to you*
If I could see you growing
I'd only be happier then
And how can I tell you I love you
If I cannot see you again
> *I want your heart to blossom*
> *I pray that your spirit accept*
> *The love that creation will show you*
> *Much more love will come to you yet*
I have left my life open
If you want to see me again
I'm hoping that one day I'll see you
And praying we'll grow as true friends

—Imelda Buckley

A Reunion Experience

Adoption reunion is a highly individual experience. There are no clear rules, and even language can be a barrier. Anyone involved in adoption reunion, whether in a personal or helping role, needs to be sensitive to the overall issues and individual differences for all parties in the adoption triangle. Adoption reunion touches many lives. The following pages describe interviews videotaped two years after a reunion that took place in 1985.

The birthmother, Donna, was 35 years old and single. Her birthson, Ken, was 16 years old. Donna placed Ken for adoption in 1969, when she was 19 years of age. (Ken is the legal name given by the adoptive parents.) Lynda and Lou adopted Ken as an infant through the Ministry of Social Services in British Columbia, Canada. Lynda had had four miscarriages. Two-and-a-half years after Ken's adoption, Lynda and Lou conceived a son, Brian.

The interviews were spontaneous, and the answers were not rehearsed or prompted in any way. The only person whom the author had met beforehand was Donna, but the other interviews were done at the time of the first meeting, so the author was unaware of their perspective until afterwards.

The videotape begins with an interview with Donna, Ken's birthmother, by the author. The second interview is with Ken's adoptive mother, Lynda, followed by an interview with Ken's adoptive father, Lou. Ken was apprehensive about being interviewed on the videotape; his perspective is summarized from an audiotaped interview.

Adoption Reunion Video

Transcript of Interview with Birthmother

Q.   What led you to begin your search for your son, Donna?

A.   I started when he was eight years old, and I went to the Ministry of Human Resources offices. I spoke to a social worker, who discouraged me from pursuing it. There really wasn't any hope of getting any information on my son at that time, so I left it. I thought it was probably better to leave it, especially as a social worker told me that I shouldn't pursue it. I thought that he knew better than I did.

So eight years went by. It was Christmas time, and there was a commercial on the TV about the Special Olympics for handicapped children. I saw this handicapped child on TV, and I said, "My gosh! What if that's my son!" It wasn't the first time that I'd wondered if my child was handicapped. But this particular day moved me to a point where I got up from the couch, and I looked up an agency that helps people search for their children. I wrote them a letter that night and mailed it the next day. On that day, at that particular Christmas time, I just felt so compelled. It had been 16 years of building up to that point, and that was the trigger that made me go forth.

Q   What was your fantasy about your son? Where did you think he was? What did you think he was doing?

A   Well, I had a few fantasies, not just one. First of all, I was convinced that my son and his family lived in the Okanagan. Somewhere along the line I was given the impression that both the adoptive parents were school teachers. I'm not sure where this information came from. I'm unsure whether it was given to me at the time of the adoption, or if I had imagined it over the course of the years because this was something that I would have wanted for him, to be in that kind of professional family.

My fantasies about Ken were mixed. Because I didn't know whether he was alive or dead, some of my fantasies were morbid in a way, because I would think, "Maybe he had died in a car accident." Of course, I didn't want to dwell on these thoughts too much, but it could have been a reality. The other fantasies were that he was very bright at school, very active and involved in sports. They were all the wonderful things that I think most parents want for their children.

Q. What were your feelings and fantasies about the adoptive parents? You've mentioned a couple; did you have any others?

A. Mostly I imagined them to be considerably older than they are. I guess that's part of the mystery of adoptive parents. I assumed that they had been married for a long time and that they had tried and tried for years to have children, and they had waited for more years for a child to come along for them to adopt. So I just assumed that they were a lot older than I. Of course that affected my perception as to what they might be like. It turned out that we are almost the same age. Ken's adoptive father Lou is only three or four years older than I. It is the same with his adoptive mother. So we're in much the same age bracket, which was very unexpected for me.

Q. How did you actually locate your son?

A. I placed an advertisement in the newspaper in the anniversary column on his 16th birthday. His birthday was at the weekend. I placed the advertisement in the Friday and Saturday night papers. I was told that this was a good step to take. The advertisement wished him birthday wishes from his birthmother. Because he was 16 years old I worded the advertisement to say "Adoptive parents please reply," rather than putting the onus on him because of his young age.

The odd thing about that was that I didn't really expect a response. I had waited 16 years for this moment to come. I put the advertisement in the paper and thought, "Well, this is the first step." Putting the advertisement in the paper was scary. I was very nervous about it. When I phoned the newspaper and told them what I wanted to put in the advertisement, I had them repeat it to me two or three times over the telephone because I thought, "They mustn't make a mistake on the birthdate or anything." I thought that maybe the following year I would try advertising again, and I would just keep doing it every year.

Q. *So you weren't anticipating that anything was going to happen the first year?*

A. No! Of course, people told me, "Now Donna, don't get your hopes up. This is just your first time so don't expect anything." There was a small part of me that thought, "Maybe," but then I thought, "No. That's not realistic." That could never happen to me.

Q. *What factors were important to you in setting up your reunion?*

A. The thing that was most important to me was that we all understood each other, and that before Ken and I saw each other, they understood my position. I wanted Ken's family to like me. I wanted them to not feel threatened by me. I wanted Ken to feel sure that he wanted to go through with actually meeting me.

Not all of this was deliberately planned. It's just that after the first contact you start thinking. Every day is another step forward, and you want it to go so well that you start thinking of things that may happen, or that you want to happen. So at the time I placed the advertisement, I didn't plan a reunion. I didn't think that far ahead. I could only think to the point of placing the advertisement. When the possibility of a reunion became a reality, then I started thinking things through because it was so important.

Q. *How did you get the first contact?*

A. A friend of Ken's mom and dad saw the advertisement in the paper and phoned them and told them about it. I'm not quite sure exactly what happened in Ken's house after they saw the advertisement. I know that it was emotional, and I know that they talked about it a lot. I also know that it was 12 days before Ken's mother made a phone call to the number I had left in the paper. It was the number of an agency I had applied to.

Q. *So by that time, you had given up hope?*

A. Oh, sure! I gave up hope the following weekend. I felt that if they had seen the advertisement they would have called immediately, and if they didn't call then, they never would call.

Q. *What happened when she phoned you?*

A. She didn't phone me. She phoned the Canadian Adoptees

Reform Association. This was the agency I had been using. I had left their box number. She phoned and talked to them. One of the volunteers from that group phoned me and said, "You'd better sit down. We've had a response to your ad!" So I did not speak to Ken's mom for about a week after that.

Q. *Did you initiate the contact with her, or did she call you?*

A. She called me. As a matter of fact, she called and left a message on my answering machine because I wasn't home. She said she would call me back in half an hour or something. I was just going nuts waiting for her to call back, and trying to compose myself!

Q. *As you reflect back now, it's been two years ago since that first contact was made, what was helpful in that process?*

A. Well, the first thing that comes to mind is Ken, and the fact that he accepted me. Secondly, the support of his mom and dad, Lynda and Lou. You can't have a one-sided reunion. It involves everyone. Unless you have total understanding, good communication, and trust, I don't think it would work. So I've tried very hard, but I know that they have tried hard too. I think that's why it's working so well.

Q. *As you look back, what was the most rewarding part of everything?*

A. I think it was knowing that Ken was okay. He has a good family and good home. He's healthy. He's not an Einstein, but he has an awful lot of other good qualities, and I think that's because of the way he has been raised. I think the most rewarding thing is knowing that he and his family are fine.

Q. *What has been the hardest part throughout all this?*

A. Dealing with my emotions. Sometimes I feel very sad. It's just this constant process of telling myself, still, that what I did was right in terms of the initial adoption. I'm also trying not to persecute myself as I did for so long. I want to enjoy my good fortune. I still have some difficulties.

There is one thing that I've not told Ken or his family, and that is that I'd really like a hug. When he was a newborn, I didn't touch him physically because it was too emotional to do that. I know he's a bit shy, but there have been some times when I'd just like to squeeze him to death. I know that he's not that type of fellow, and I wouldn't impose on him and make him feel uncomfortable. But now I understand when my mom wants to just hug me to death. It's a really neat thing to want to do.

Q.   *Now that all of this is coming out for you in your life—the secret of having placed a child for adoption—you have to explain to people Ken's part in your life. How has that been for you, that the secret is kind of coming out of the closet?*

A.   When you asked me to be a part of this presentation, my first reaction was, "My gosh, I'm going public!" I immediately thought of Alcoholics Anonymous. I think that in some ways being a birthmother is a more secret organization than something like that. I'm trying to be more open about it, but it's difficult because for 16 years I wasn't open about it. Those were my growing-up years and my early twenties when I never dealt with it. So there were 16 years of my life where that was a secret. It's difficult, in two years, to all of a sudden deal with it properly and be able to talk about it comfortably and openly. I still have some things I want to resolve so it will take time. But I find too, that sometimes I wish my friends and my family would ask me more often how Ken is doing.

Q.   *What has been the reaction of your family and friends?*

A.   They have been very supportive. The relationship with my parents since the reunion has changed dramatically. We're much closer because we finally talked about this and shared our feelings; we just misunderstood each other for many, many years and if we hadn't had the reunion we may have kept on that way.

Q.   *So it's worked out in a positive way with your family?*

A.   Yes, I think so.

Q.   *What was their reaction to meeting Ken?*

A.   Well, I was very hesitant to share my news with my parents. I was afraid of their reaction. Sadly, they were the last people I shared my news with because I thought it would be really difficult. Of course, they surprised me. They were wonderfully supportive and excited. All those years when I thought my mom and dad weren't interested and didn't care about Ken, my mother had been remembering his birthday every year and looking at advertisements in the paper to see if there was anything about him.

Q.   *But she had never said anything to you?*

A.   No, and I never said anything to her. She thought that because I didn't talk about it, that I didn't care. I thought that because she never asked me about it, that she didn't care. And so for all those years we had this misunderstanding, which was so silly!

Q.   *What are the issues that you are now having to face?*

A. I think one of the most difficult things right now is identifying myself as a birthmother. In a group of people, I find the question, "Do you have any children, Donna?" very difficult to answer. I'm very proud of my experience, and I'm very proud of Ken and his family. I would like to share that feeling more. When somebody says, " Do you have any children, Donna?" I'd like to be able to say, "Yes I do." I'd like to feel proud about it in a group of people without fear of them judging me or them dropping their mouths in horror or disbelief. I get the feeling that, generally speaking, it's not something you can just blurt out.

Q. *Have you any other things that you are still having to deal with as you work all this into your life?*

A. Mostly my ability to recognize Ken as a part of my life. I do that to a certain degree, but I would like more acknowledgment. I'd like to be able to work on that somehow.

Q. *How has all this affected you personally, and how you feel about yourself?*

A. Well, initially my friends thought that I had done the silliest thing in the world, because at the beginning, the emotional impact was devastating. I cried. I didn't sleep. I messed up at work. I just went bouncing off walls the first few months. The emotion was incredible, and I didn't know how to handle it. At that time I didn't have too much support from other people who had been through this experience.

Now, two years later, I'm of course becoming more comfortable with it, and I'm becoming more confident about our reunion. I feel as if I've grown up. I feel that I kind of coasted along in my life, not taking any chances, not moving forward, just staying at the same level. Especially in this last year I feel I have matured. I've made some changes in my life. There seems to be an awful lot going on in my life right now, where for years there wasn't. I think that my confidence has improved, because I'm not running myself down as much any more with those thoughts I used to have about my son, wondering what I'd done or where he was. Those thoughts have a very negative impact on your life after 16 years. I think it affects your character and your personality. Since the reunion, it's been such a happy experience all around, I'm starting to feel better inside, about it all.

Q. *If you had to do it all over again, would you do anything differently?*

A. I'm fairly pleased with the way it all went. I think if I had to do it all over again, I'd tell my parents first. That's the only thing I would change.

Transcript of Interview with Adoptive Mother

Q. Lynda, what was your initial reaction when you saw the advertisement in the newspaper?
A. It shocked me. I also thought it was pretty neat, and I was dying to get home and talk to Ken about it.

Q. How did you find out about it?
A. My girlfriend phoned me at work. There was an advertisement in the paper for her husband's birthday. So when she phoned me and asked me if I'd read the paper, it was because she had seen another advertisement, and it was from Ken's birthmother.

Q. Did you ever think you would see an advertisement in the paper?
A. No. We'd never paid any attention to these advertisements. It's just not something we ever thought about.

Q. So your first reaction was to go and tell Ken?
A. Yes.

Q. What was his reaction?
A. The same way. It's always been very open in our house, so when I came home from work I said to Ken, "You're not going to believe this!" Of course, I bought a paper on my way home from work, and I said to him, "Listen to this ad." He read it and said, "Holy cow! This could be for me!" That was the start of it, and I said, "Yes, and what are we going to do about it?" So actually, between all of us, we just worked together and ran through it as we went.

Q. What was the next step?
A. The next day I phoned the Ministry of Human Resources to try to find out if there was a way I could find out anything about Ken's birthparents. I got a very cold response from them. They didn't feel they could help me, but they said they would give me a call back when they had checked into it. I've never received a call back, and it's been over two years now.

Q. What did you do when you didn't receive any information from them?
A. When I realized they were so negative about it, I phoned Burnaby General Hospital. I got lucky, because I ended up speaking to a woman who was really understanding. I asked her if there

was any way she could tell me how many boys were born on that day and how many were given up for adoption. A few days later she was able to get back to me to tell me that three boys were born on that date, and two were given up for adoption. From there, we proceeded further.

Q. *How did you find out which one was your son?*

A. We wrote a letter to the box number that was in the paper saying what I had done up to that point, that there were two boys who were born that day, and that I had the birthmother's birthdate. I asked her if she would put her birthdate in the paper to confirm that she was the real birthmother.

While we were waiting for a response in the paper, I saw another ad with the same box number, but it also had a phone number. It was the Canadian Adoptees Reform Association. I phoned there, not knowing who they were. I was a little leery that they were trying to take my son for some weird reason. I phoned and talked to them and eventually through a process of elimination, they finally gave me Donna's birthdate. It was the exact birthdate, and then from there, everything pointed to the fact that she had to be Ken's birthmother.

Q. *What was your fantasy about Ken's birthparents? What kind of people they might be, or what they might look like?*

A. I never thought about their looks or anything. I knew the basics, that the birthmother was pregnant and as soon as the boyfriend knew she was pregnant he left and went to Europe. Other than that, I'd like to believe that she gave Ken up because she felt he would have a better chance in an adopted home rather than trying to look after him herself. I tried to instill in Ken that she loved him enough to give him up.

Q. *Did you have any fears after you read that advertisement and started to think through what it meant?*

A. Not initially. Initially it was fine. I felt that it was just great. Once it had come to the point where we were going to write a letter, then I felt a little hesitant. I was slowing down. I was starting to realize that there was a little part of me that said, "They're taking part of my kid away." I was scared of that a little bit. Yet the other part of me knew that I had no concerns there. So I was struggling with that.

My husband was very much for Donna. As soon as it came up, he said, "Now she knows we're here, we have to respond. Come on!

Hurry up." Later on, once I met Donna, I was fine. That's when Lou backed off. He would say, "I don't know about this whole situation," and he was putting the brakes on. So I guess we had our different emotions at different times.

Q.   *How did the first meeting with Donna take place. Were you the first one to make contact with her?*

A.   Yes. We wrote her a letter. Basically, I wrote it and Ken and Lou read it. We all agreed on it, then we mailed it. I had to take away some of the stuff because Ken figured I was being too mushy. We did it back and forth like that. I sent the letter to the Canadian Adoptees Reform group, and then Donna sent me a letter back. I sent her a picture of Ken, who was 16 at that time, and also a baby picture of him.

After a couple of letters we made a decision that we were going to meet. I was going to meet her at her house on a Sunday afternoon. I took along all our baby pictures and all kinds of family photo albums and as much stuff as I thought she might be interested in. I went to her house. It was a very choked-up, emotional thing the first time we met. When I met her we just both started to cry. I wanted nothing but good from it, but my biggest concern was always how Ken was going to come out of all of this. He was 16 years old, and we didn't want him to have any more problems than he already had as an adolescent.

Q.   *What factors were important to you from your perspective as an adoptive mother, when you were setting up this reunion?*

A.   The number one thing was Ken. I always did feel that we had always handled the adoption issue in our house very well. We also have a biological child who is two-and-a-half years younger than Ken. I guess I wanted to make sure that we all stayed together as a family unit, and we went through this situation in a way that no one was left out.

Q.   *As you look back now over the last couple of years, what was the most rewarding part in all of it?*

A.   I think that Ken feels much more trust in us. I think he felt very good that we trusted him enough to work through this information with him at his age, rather than holding it back. I think, as an adolescent, although he didn't really question it all that much, I think he found answers to questions he didn't know he had. I think it helped him identify who he really was. With the difficulties of being a 16-year-old, I think it somehow in many ways made it easier when he had this kind of background. I think he can honestly look at Donna, and it feels good because Donna looks a lot like him. I think that is kind of nice for Ken; I think he likes that.

Q. *Are there personality traits that they have in common?*

A. Oh yes, lots! I see it so often, the silliest things that make you wonder how it happens. How can they have the same habit of twitching their nose? They've never been together, and yet there are certain things like that they do. There are certain character traits and some flaws that make me think, "Oh, where does he get them from?" I now know, and I don't feel guilty because I didn't give them to him!

Q. *What was the hardest part, Lynda, with all this, for you as a mother?*

A. I guess as a mother, you feel it's possession, and it isn't. I think it made me aware that Ken is not my possession. Because using the term "my son" made me think of him as mine, and every now and then, Donna would use the same term, "my son." That can sometimes choke me. Somehow I feel, "No. You haven't got that right." I feel for her in some respects, and I have nothing but good thoughts about her, but there is a part of me that says, "Eighteen years I've been his mother. He's ours." You go through the good times as well as the bad and the difficult together and somehow you say, "When you're sitting up all night worrying about where he is or why he isn't home, that's who the mother is."

But Donna is being very mature about it. She's never wanted to be his mom. That's not what she's after. She's just wanted to find out what happened to him and where he was, and to share just a part of his life and family.

Q. *There's no good language, is there, to describe the relation-ships?*

A. No. It's something unique and new. I think it's really good that people are being made aware that it has to be dealt with. More and more of this is going to happen. We had nowhere to go when all of a sudden we had this ad, and we were not trained in any way, shape, or form as to what to do. You just have to figure it out in your own mind and how you know your kid, and what's the best thing to do. It's not easy. Once you're faced with that ad, you have to deal with it.

Q. *Are there any things now, two years later, that you are still having to deal with as a family or by yourself?*

A.   I don't always know how much or how little contact we should have. I don't want to be a nuisance to her any more than I want to always have to worry about phoning her, but I think she feels the same way. I think as time goes by and the years go by, we will gradually get a better, comfortable feeling about that. So far, it's been good. Sometimes I think maybe Donna would like to see more of Ken, and I have no objection to it. But I get busy with my life, and I don't really walk around thinking about it.

Q.   *You were telling me that he spontaneously went to Donna's with his girlfriend recently?*

A.   Yes, just last week. I thought it was really neat for Donna because up until then, I would phone, or Donna would phone, and if Ken is around he would talk to her on the phone or we'd get together for coffee. But last Monday, Ken was saying that he went riding on his motorcycle with his girlfriend. He said, "Guess where we went yesterday? We dropped by Donna's." I thought that was really neat. I haven't talked to Donna yet, but I'm sure she probably thought it was great.

Q.   *So for the first time it came from him?*

A.   That's what he decided to do that afternoon, and it had nothing to do with me. I didn't even know until a day later when he happened to mention it.

Transcript of Interview with Adoptive Father

Q.   *Lou, what was your initial reaction when you heard about the advertisement? Your wife said she saw the ad, then she mentioned it to Ken.*

A.   It was quite a shock actually, because we had never dreamed it would happen that way. We had never thought of looking in the paper before, or anything like that. I found it interesting for Ken's sake, because he was never really searching, but he was always curious. I thought this was a chance for him to follow up his curiosity.

Q.   *Had he asked very much over the years?*

A.   Not really. It has always been an open topic. When we did talk about it, he always expressed a mild curiosity. He had said before that, he wouldn't mind peeking through a keyhole or checking her out from a distance, but he had never really expressed any desire to go looking for her or knocking on her door.

Q.   *How did your first meeting with Donna take place? Lynda said that she went to Donna's apartment with some pictures. How did you first meet Donna?*

A. We met a while later at a restaurant in Burnaby. It went pretty well actually. Lynda went to the washroom just at the wrong time and left me all alone when Donna came in, and I felt really silly. I saw this woman come in and look around, and I thought this must be her, so I just introduced myself. It went really well. We sat around and had a few drinks and talked for the longest time. It was a good meeting. I was rather pleased with it.

Q. *How did Ken's meeting with Donna take place? How was it set up?*

A. Lynda set it up with Donna. She brought him over to Donna's apartment and dropped him off there and arranged to pick him up later. She then came home and proceeded to cry over at the neighbor's house for the whole afternoon, and picked him up later. It went pretty well, I think, and Ken enjoyed it.

Q. *Did he express any apprehension before he went?*

A. Not too much. Every time it comes up, I'm always amazed about how cool he is about the whole thing. He usually avoids awkward situations, but when it comes to his birthmother, he has always been quite open about it. If it were me, I would have been much more apprehensive than he was.

Q. *Did he say anything after he came back from his first visit? I guess you were all waiting to see how it went.*

A. I don't recall exactly what he said about it, but I think it was positive. He was quite pleased with the meeting.

Q. *What was the reaction of family and friends to all this? How did your relatives react?*

A. They were more apprehensive than we were, but I think they could afford to be because they could just stand back and say, "I'd be careful of that if I were you." They would just leave it at that, but we couldn't say that, because we had to deal with Ken all the time. When it first came up, we didn't have a whole lot of choice but to follow it through, because we had always been very open with Ken about his adoption. Once we saw the ad we just had to follow it through, wherever it led us. We have been really fortunate the way it all worked out.

Q. *So it seems that the decision to pursue it was an easy one to make?*

A. It wasn't even a decision. We had to do it. We didn't have a choice there. How to pursue it was something else. Lynda was a little slow at first, and then later on, I was a little more hesitant, but we slowly worked our way through it all. It worked really well.

Q. *What advice did you get from relatives and well-meaning individuals?*

A. It was not really advice. They would throw little things into the works like, "You don't know what you're getting into," or "You don't know what she's like. You don't want her on your doorstep all the time." Little tidbits like that, but they would never go further than that.

Q. *What do they think now that Donna has met with you and Ken?*

A. They have accepted it. My brother, his wife and kids, and our friends are quite accepting of it. They are quite curious about it. My mother and Lynda's mother hardly talk about it at all. They are a little more possessive that way. Maybe they're from the old school that adoption wasn't really "in" in those days, and maybe they don't consider that an adopted child is the same as a real child.

Q. *So you're not sure what values they hold. They don't say too much?*

A. It's hard to say. You really don't know how anyone else feels. They don't dislike Ken or treat him any differently. They just don't talk of the fact that his birthmother is "in the wings" somewhere.

Q. *So you know that just by the fact that they don't talk about it, that they are a little bit sensitive for some reason?*

A. That's right. I think it might be because they came from Holland. In Holland, when they were our age, they never had an adoption system. I don't think you could ever really legally adopt, it was more of a fostering system they had. It wasn't the same as it is here.

Summary of Interview with Adopted Son

Ken was 18 years of age at the time of this interview. His general attitude about the reunion was casual and low key. In fact he was the most relaxed person in the triangle. He felt that overall it was a positive experience that was hard to put into words.

When his parents showed him the advertisement, he did not believe it at first. He thought that maybe it was the birthmother of another child adopted that day from the hospital. It did not sink in until the last minute when his mom was actually in contact with Donna.

Over the years, Ken had not thought much about his birthparents. He had no visual image of them. He knew his birthmother was unmarried and too young to look after him properly. His parents had always been open about the adoption and told him that his birthmother must have cared for him a lot. Ken's last-minute fear before meeting Donna was, "What if this lady turns out to be weird?"

Ken did not worry too much about his parents' reaction because he figured that they could handle it, but the possible reaction of his grandmother crossed his mind. Ken would have liked to have been the first to meet Donna. He felt that his parents were leery about the situation, and feared that this lady might have come to take him back. So he figured that it worked out best for his family to have his mom and dad meet Donna first. After Lynda's meeting with Donna, Ken felt relieved to hear his mom speak positively about his birthmother. He saw two pictures of Donna and felt it was like looking at pictures of someone he did not know.

Ken was nervous at the time of his first meeting with Donna and felt unsure about what to say. At first he did not see his resemblance with Donna, but then the first thing he felt that they had in common was their stubborn nature. He felt that it was neat to see himself mirrored in another person whom he had not known for 16 years, and then to meet even more people in her family. He felt it was special to be the only grandchild in Donna's family. The genetic similarity made an impression on him.

Ken felt that the reaction of his friends was positive. All his friends have liked Donna. They tell Ken that Donna looks and acts like him.

Ken felt that there was nothing very difficult about the reunion other than his problem describing his relationship with Donna to others. He refers to Donna as his "real mom" when he is talking with his friends, because he feels that this most easily explains their relationship. He feels that friends would not understand if he were to say that he was going to Donna's place. He realizes that this makes his parents feel awkward. When he is around his parents, he feels he has to use certain words. Ken feels that people should not get too hung up about the reunion and should not get too uptight over the language. It bothers him when people refer to others as a possession, as in "my son."

Ken does not feel that this experience has changed him or

altered how he feels about himself. He seems to have a good sense of his own identity and is able to cope with difference. In fact, he seems to like being different because it has a special quality. This may have been a real strength for Ken in the adoption and reunion.

The reunion brought up questions for Ken that he had never thought of before. Yes, he would do it all over again. He felt that meeting Donna was a positive experience. He described the reunion as an interesting and quite enjoyable experience. He feels that it would have been ridiculous to have made him wait until the age of majority to meet his birthmother if she was looking for him.

Ken says that he is not the emotional type, so reunion was not an overwhelmingly emotional experience for him. It opened up a new area for him because he has found it interesting to see how others reacted to this reunion experience, such as family, friends, and society. He expressed an interest in working in a field where he could help others.

Ken sees his relationship with Donna as being like that of an aunt. He wants to continue seeing Donna. Their visits average about every two to three months, with some phone contact.

❖❖❖❖❖

This is an example of a positive reunion experience. All the individuals involved put a tremendous amount of effort and energy into planning and communicating with one another. They took it slowly and were sensitive to each other's needs. Both the birthmother and the adoptive parents tried hard to put Ken's needs first, rather than their own. It was a pleasure to have the opportunity to interview Donna, Lynda, Lou, and Ken because they were so open and honest. It was a truly a learning experience for me.

9
When Do You Need Outside Help?

It is always difficult to ask others for help, but there are times when you will need someone to lean on. Experiencing loss is one of the times when you will need people—family, friends, spouse or boyfriend—around you for support, comfort, and understanding. One good, sensitive friend can make all the difference in the world.

There are times, however, when you may well need help from a professional who is more emotionally detached from your situation and able to be an objective counselor or consultant. Sometimes family and friends are not available to you as supports, or you may not want to burden them with your problems. Other times they offer well-meaning advice that may be insensitive, such as, "You can always have more children," or "You did the right thing," or "You'll forget in time and get on with your life." Friends and family may have difficulty offering support because of biases or emotional closeness. Some people find it easier to share problems with a professional helper because they cannot talk to anyone they know about the confusing feelings of pain, hurt, shame, or guilt. Only you can decide what is best for you at any given time; just be aware that people are available to help if you take the time to look.

What Is Counseling All About?

Seeking help is not a sign of weakness but rather a sign that you have the strength to identify your emotional needs and reach out to get those needs met. It is a sign of coping, because you are searching for ways to look after yourself and are striving for emotional health, rather than letting yourself head for a crisis.

You do not have to have serious emotional problems to ask for help; professional counseling can be preventive and supportive. The counselor is there to act as a listener, a sounding board, and an emotional guide, to help you think through problems and find alternate ways to deal with the situations that you face, not to give you advice on the best way to handle a situation.

85

A counselor's training may be in nursing, social work, psychology, or psychiatry. These professionals work in a variety of settings such as adoption agencies, mental health clinics, private offices, adolescent clinics, schools, women's health centers, social service organizations, family counseling agencies, and hospitals. If you do seek help from a professional, it is important to find a person to whom you can relate. Remember also that help is available from the clergy and volunteer organizations.

As in any kind of work or profession, counselors vary in ability, amount of experience, and in their special areas of experience. If a counselor proves unhelpful to you for any reason, you have the right to look for another agency or counselor who meets your needs. It is important to find someone who understands what birthparent grief is all about, and who is sensitive about the impact it has had on your life.

Another type of help available is that of support groups consisting of people who have gone through similar experiences. The adoptees' reform movement led the way in the organization of such groups, and they are expanding. You may feel more comfortable talking with someone who has experienced placing a child for adoption than talking with a friend, family member, or a professional. Others who have "been there before" can readily understand your feelings. They can provide a support network out of which deep friendships can emerge. You will find that you are not alone.

> *Donna:* Oh how I wish that I'd found a support group sooner. I believe that my life would have been a lot different because the group has helped me know that I am a good person.

There are also organizations that you can join for a membership fee, such as Concerned United Birthparents or the American Adoption Congress. These organizations have chapter meetings in various districts, sponsor conferences, and publish informative newsletters. The newsletters are one way to keep in touch with changes in legislation, current issues, and personal stories, and they have advice columns for the members. So there are many avenues to a kind of help and support that fits for you.

> *Pauline:* With the support groups, workshops, and coun-

seling sessions, I am learning about my feelings about my pregnancy and adoption, and how they affected my life. It's painful digging up these emotions, and I feel drained after the sessions, but the results have been positive.

Where Can You Find Help?

There are various social service organizations listed in your phone directory that offer counseling. If you are unsure where to turn, the crisis line in your community is a good beginning. Crisis lines are available 24 hours a day and refer you to appropriate resources for help. They are a good resource when you feel overwhelmed, have no idea where to turn for help, or just need a listening ear.

Other social service organizations that may be resources for you include the adoption agency, Children's Aid Society, family service organization, department of social services, family doctor, mental health clinic, hospital social work department, clergy, public health unit, women's center, school or university counseling service, teen clinic, health center, grief and loss counseling center, home for unwed mothers, YWCA, Planned Parenthood, or professionals in private practice such as psychiatrists, social workers, or psychologists.

North American organizations—those who have shared in the adoption experience—include Concerned United Birthparents and American Adoption Congress (both mentioned above), Parent Finders, Birthparent Support Network, and many adoptees' activist groups and search and reunion registries.

Concerned United Birthparents (CUB) deserves special comment because it was the first birthparent activist group formed. Established in 1976, CUB now has chapters all over North America. The group's aim is to help both birthmothers and birthfathers cope with the feelings and adjustments related to relinquishment. CUB publishes a wide variety of resource material available for birthparents at minimal cost, and operates a reunion registry. CUB has been a major support in uniting birthparents across Canada and the United States, and has helped birthparents to come out of the closet without shame.

Resources for Seeking Help and Support

Organizations

Family Service America

> 11700 West Lake Park Drive
> Park Place
> Milwaukee, WI, USA 53224
> (414) 359–2111
> (FSA has 280 local family service agencies in Canada and USA)

Child Welfare League of America

> 440 First Street, N.W., Suite 310
> Washington, DC, USA 20001
> (202) 638-2952
> (CWLA can provide information about counseling resources and adoption agencies in your community)

Concerned United Birthparents, Inc.

> 2000 Walker Street
> Des Moines, IA, USA 50317
> President: Carole Anderson
> (319) 359–4068

American Adoption Congress

> Box 44040
> L'Enfant Plaza
> Washington, DC, USA 22026-0040
> (505) 296–2198

Birthparent Support Network

> Box 120
> N. White Plains, NY, USA 10603
> Executive Editor of *The Network News*: Gail Davenport
> (914) 682–2250

Adoption Options Newsletter

> Room 30
> 7340 —78 Street
> Edmonton, Alberta, Canada T6C 2N1

The Triad Tribune (TRIAD Society for Truth in Adoption)

> Triad of Canada
> Box 5922, Station B
> Victoria, B.C.
> Canada V8R 6S8
> (604) 598-9887

Adoption Reunion Registries:

Adoption reunion registries allow for the exchange of identifying information when the birthparent and adult adoptee have both registered. Some registries permit relatives other than birthparents and adoptees to register.

There are two types of reunion registries: active and passive registries. A passive registry allows for the exchange of information only after both parties have voluntarily registered with the same registry. An active registry searches on behalf of the registering party. Some registries will search only on behalf of the adult adoptee, but some will search on behalf of the birthparent. You will need to find out if there is a registry in your community.

United States.

In the United States the main registry is called "Soundex." There are other smaller registries, but this registry is recommended. You can register in as many registries operated by private groups as you desire. Soundex has no fee for registration and does not provide search assistance.

International Soundex Reunion Registry

> P.O. Box 2312
> Carson City, NV, USA 89702

There are many independent organizations such as ALMA (Adoptees Liberation Movement Association) that operate registries, provide search assistance, and often have lending libraries. A fee is usually involved. If you require search assistance, CUB provides a list of organizations in the USA, Australia, England, and New Zealand that can assist you.

Canada

In Canada, reunion registries are under provincial jurisdiction. You can register only in the province where you placed your baby for adoption. Policies of reunion registries vary widely from province to province. Some registries have a fee for registering, for providing nonidentifying information or for searching, while others are free of charge. Many provincial registries have a work backlog, and it can take several months for a response for nonidentifying information or for a search to begin.

Some independent organizations, such as "Parent Finders," operate reunion registries, provide search assistance, and often have lending libraries. A fee is usually involved for registering with an independent organization.

British Columbia (passive registry)

Division of Vital Statistics
Adoption Reunion Registry
1515 Blanshard Street
Victoria, BC, Canada V8W 3C8

Alberta (passive registry)

Alberta Social Services
12th Floor
Seventh Street Plaza
10030 107 Street
Edmonton, Alberta, Canada T5J 3E4

Saskatchewan (active registry for adult adoptees and passive registry for birthparents)

Post Adoption Services
2240 Albert Street
Regina, Saskatchewan, Canada S4S 3V7

Manitoba (active registry for adult adoptees and passive registry for birthparents)

Adoption Registry Coordinator
Manitoba Community Services
2nd Floor
114 Garry Street
Winnipeg, Manitoba, Canada R3C 1G1

Ontario (active registry for adult adoptees and passive registry for birthparents)

Adoption Disclosure Registry
Children's Services Branch
Community Services Division
2nd Floor
700 Bay Street
Toronto, Ontario, Canada M5G 1Z6

Quebec (active registry for adult adoptees and birthparents of an adult adoptee)

The Adoption Secretariat
3700 Berri Street
Montreal, Quebec, Canada, H2L 4G9

New Brunswick (passive registry)

Postadoption Services
Dept. of Health and Community Services
P.O. Box 5100
Fredericton, New Brunswick, Canada E3B 5G8

Newfoundland (passive registry)

Coordinator, Postadoption Services
Box 4750
St. John's, Newfoundland, Canada A1C 5T7

Nova Scotia (passive registry)

Director of Family and Children's Services
Dept. of Social Services
P.O. Box 696
Halifax, Nova Scotia, Canada B3J 2T7

Prince Edward Island (no registry in legislation; send letter indicating desire for reunion)

> Dept. of Health and Social Services
> P.O. Box 2000
> Charlottetown, P.E.I., Canada C1A 7N8

Yukon (passive registry)

> Director of Family and Children's Services
> P.O. Box 2703
> Whitehorse, Yukon, Canada Y1A 2C6

Northwest Territories (no registry in legislation; send letter indicating desire for reunion)

> Superintendant of Child Welfare
> 6th Floor, Precambrian Building
> Yellowknife, N.W.T., Canada X1A 2L9